Brothers at Daybreak

**World War II B-24 crew
beats the odds
over Pacific waters**

Their story as told to
Virginia C. McPartland

Brothers at Daybreak

ISBN: 978-1-61170-127-2

Library of Congress Control Number: 2013942299

Printed in the USA and UK on acid-free paper.

Robertson Publishing™
www.RobertsonPublishing.com

To purchase additional copies of this book go to:
amazon.com
barnesandnoble.com

FOREWORD

As a B-24 bomber crew in the Pacific during World War II, we were very unusual because we had our own Keystone 8mm movie camera, thanks to pilot Frank Jeter.

We took turns filming action shots during our bombing missions and recorded scenes of our life on the ground. The undeveloped film escaped the censors and came home with us as a rare memento of our experience.

The Jeter Crew flew 37 combat missions in the Western Pacific, China and Japan. We received the Distinguished Flying Cross, five air medals and medals for the following campaigns: Action in the Western Pacific, Air Combat Iwo Jima, Air Combat Ryukyus, Air Offense China and Air Offense Japan.

E. John Weller
Navigator
The Jeter Crew

My father, a World War II veteran, died in 2002. I knew that he had participated in the war but the details were sketchy. Honestly, up until he got sick I had little interest. I never asked him a single question about the war until the Christmas before he suffered a debilitating episode that left him like a child and uncommunicative. He had never offered one solitary war story, joyful or horrendous, for the entire five decades that we were in one another's life.

Growing up in California, I learned a bit about the war in school. It was in Europe and Asia. We dropped nuclear bombs on Japan, two acts whose legitimacy scholars endlessly debated. We defeated Germany and Japan and our lives were good after that, except for the Cold War that kept us at odds with the Russians and Chinese. Until recently, I had no idea that the Russians and Chinese had been our allies during World War II, an irony that continues to amaze me.

As young adults, my sisters and I used to argue with my parents about the U.S. war in Vietnam, and we could never understand why they were so worried about the Communists taking over the world. In a way, we were blissfully free of the encumbrance of having experienced the drama and loss of war and the fear of monsters like Hitler and Hirohito edging into the Free World.

In 2004, I got to know a woman who, like me, had come from a family of seven children with a dad who survived the war. Her father had won medals while in the European Theater in 1944-45, but came home angry and mean. This 50-year-old woman had many demons—she was afraid of bushes, camouflage clothing, telephone booths, and many other things. She blamed it on her parents, especially on her father who drank too much and beat her and her sisters. She is haunted by the memory of a late rainy night when she and her sister brought their pet dog inside and set up a warm and dry bed for him in the kitchen. They put up a portable gate to keep the dog from wandering around the house. Unfortunately, they woke up their father who came into the kitchen to investigate and tripped on the gate. He was so angry he beat the dog to death in the girls' presence and threw him in the garbage can.

The sad woman's story made me curious. Is it possible that soldiers who become absorbed in the brutality of war and their job of killing come home with more violent natures than when they left? Maybe such a mental state only afflicts people who had a bad childhood or who were already mentally unstable. Or could the mental trauma of facing the death and destruction of war, and then repressing the guilt and pain, be to blame for much of the alcoholism, divorce and domestic violence in today's American life? A big question!

First, I wanted to know more about what my dad did in the war. I knew he was on a bomber in the Pacific. But did he have to kill anyone? What burden of guilt might he have carried into civilian life? He was a wonderful father and man. He always tried to do the right thing. He was resourceful, strong and kind. I only saw him lose control and hit one of us a very few times. And the hurt was only minor and temporary. In his later years, after his mind was not functioning properly, his war fears re-surfaced. He used to wake my mother up during the night and ask her if she could help him on the next day's mission. He told her he was afraid he couldn't get the crew where they needed to go. Not on his own. Another time, he raced into the room in a wheelchair shouting: "Get out of here. This place is on fire!"

After my father died, I started asking my mom questions. She didn't meet my dad until after the war, but I thought he would have shared something of his war experiences with her. She remembered some things he had told her, but she didn't like to talk about the war, a sad time for her. She had lost her first husband in April of 1945 in Germany. He was 19 and was shot by a sniper on April 26 near Nuremberg when the war was technically over. She told me the story about the pony-tailed Western Union lady named Zelda who rode her bicycle around my mom's small Iowa town delivering missing-in-action and killed-in-action messages. "We always knew when we saw her coming that someone was going to be sad," said my mom who worked in the local downtown drugstore. "Then one day she came to my house. I became hysterical and Doc Dingman gave me a heavy dose of Belladonna to make me sleep."

In 2007, I was watching public television when I came across a documentary about the Jeter Crew and their emergency landing on Iwo Jima in 1945. I knew my dad had been a B-24 navigator in the Pacific so I watched with interest and then went on the film Web site for more details. I saw John Weller's name and realized he was living in San Jose, California, only about 40 miles from my Oakland home. I looked up his phone number and wrote it down but didn't try to make contact. (For more about the documentary, see Chapter 10)

After my mother died in 2009, I found documents and mementos from the war among my parents' things. One of the most exciting items was the Purple Heart my mother's first husband was awarded posthumously. The next most thrilling piece was a short story my father wrote shortly after the war. To my mind, the story is a thinly veiled first person account of my father's struggle to get the B-24 crew from Johnston Island to Kwajalein. "Bill," the fictional navigator, sweats for hours trying hard not to show any lack of confidence in his navigational skills to his crewmates. (See Appendix A for the short story.)

My sister Pat produced another piece of evidence about my father's war experience: a letter my dad had written Pat after she gave him a book about World War II aircraft for Christmas. He wrote:

"Dear Pat, I'm happy to get the pictures of the airplanes that we used to fight WW2. I was the navigator on a B-24. We used a B-24 on all of the missions of our outfit. All missions were over the Pacific Ocean where you saw nothing but ocean and a few ships. We lived on the island of Guam. We went on one-day missions and returned to our base the same day. Some days we were in the air for 17 hours.

"We had a deal. If we did 40 missions, we could go home to

the USA to stay. We did the missions and they took us home on a ship. While on the ship we learned from a radio that President Roosevelt had died. Thanks very much for all of the pictures and the book. Pop."

This was good information, but I wanted to know more. I called John Weller and found a willing informant. From him I learned that my dad had inhabited the same Pacific War universe as Frank Jeter's group. They were camped on Guam the same time as my dad, had gone through training on Oahu close to the same time as my dad and had bombed the same Pacific targets as my dad. John invited me to come down to San Jose to meet him and his wife Jo, and to pick his brain. So began the process of getting to know the Jeter Crew members, those living and those that had already gone.

As a baby boomer born in 1951, I came of age in the late 1960s and early 1970s. Away from home for the first time at 18, I thought wearing black armbands and boycotting class to go to a peace rally was routine. Surely, everyone did this as a freshman in college. I imagine that the Jeter Crew boys, so far away from home for the first time, may have thought going to war was routine, something everybody did. They were naïve babies with *everything* to lose! For them, Nietzsche was right: if the war didn't kill them, it would make them stronger. I believe this was the bottom line for the Jeter Crew, and for those like my dad who made it back to the good old US of A by the seat of their skivvies.

One of the first things John Weller said to me when I met him: "If we would have had GPS technology (global positioning system) during the war, our jobs would have been a lot easier." Navigation over the vast Pacific Ocean was a major challenge for the best trained Air Corps men. Most schools stateside taught navigation skills that would keep the guiding airman in good stead over land, such as in Europe where landmarks were abundant. But ocean navigation was an entirely new ball game. My dad taught dead reckoning at Kelly Field in Texas, but when he got to Oahu, he had to learn new methods suitable for long, sea flights. Nobody wanted to get lost and perish like Amelia Earhart and her navigator had done in 1937 in similar South Pacific territory. Ocean navigation involved taking readings from the sun during the day and from the stars at night. (Years later, my dad would consult the stars whenever he got lost driving at night.)

These Army Air Corps flyers didn't have the advantage of many technological advancements considered routine by today's Air Force. Radar was new and still being tested; the B-24 cabin was not pressurized so at routine altitudes temperatures dropped below freezing; airmen were not knowledgeable about the effects of the newly discovered "jet stream" (air currents at high altitudes above the ocean) that affected aircraft speed and fuel usage in certain places in the Pacific.

The surviving Jeter Crew members have generously shared their stories with me and offered enlightening material that helped me to know my dad better and to feel more resolved about how he experienced the war and lived his life afterwards. I've enjoyed the process of getting to know these men, and I feel like I have bonded with them, even though I only met the deceased members through their families and other crew members.

These men, products of the Great Depression and the Second World War, came home to a different world. Prosperity had returned, and people were reaping the benefits. War veterans got married, went to college, and had babies. Lost life was being replaced and bad times forgotten. Three of the Jeter Crew members became builders—Frank Jeter, Vic Crowell and Bob Larson became successful as contractors who erected homes and commercial structures to keep up with postwar growth. Late in life, Vic fulfilled his life-long ambition to become a pilot. Ray Fritter became a Catholic priest who spent his life ministering to prisoners and parish families; Greg Babykin and Sam Tillery stayed in the military, got their pilot's licenses and contributed to the technological explosion that led to our high-tech defense and space program and our electronic society; Dick David, Herb Harter, and John Weller went into business, Dick as an international banker, Herb as an insurance agent and John as marketing manager for a big paper company. Dale Henderson became a history teacher and was active in Oregon politics; Doyle Ebel became a well-respected petrochemical fire fighter and expert.

The four Texans, Frank, Herb, Vic and Doyle went back to Texas; Sam found life pleasant in Hawaii so he settled his family in the tropical paradise rather than staying in Arkansas; Dick slipped right back into his banking career in Chicago; and John and Ray returned to their native California. Bob Larson, from Arlington, SD, had left home at 14 and first settled after the war in California, and then in Oregon.

All the Jeter Crew men, except Ray, got married and had children. Seven stayed happily married throughout the years; three were divorced from their first wives and remarried. (Bob wins the prize for the most children: he had seven sons.) Two crew members died in their 60s: Ray of liver cancer at 63 in 1985; Frank of leukemia at 66 in 1989. Vic, the youngest, died of bladder cancer at 76 in 2001; Dale of bone cancer at 79 in 2002; Greg passed away in 2009 at age 86; Bob, the oldest, died of Parkinson's Disease at 90 in 2011. Doyle and Sam, both 88, and John, Herb, and Dick, all 89, are still telling their war stories as of this writing.

Part 1

The Jeter Crew's
tour of duty in the Pacific
Theater of World War II

Brothers at Daybreak

The Frank Jeter Crew

Eleven American boys from various backgrounds found themselves together as a B-24 bomber crew in the Pacific Theater of World War II. Here they are in February of 1945 on the island of Saipan where they staged bombing raids against Japanese-held territories. Iwo Jima, site of some of the bloodiest battles in the war, looms large in this crew's experience, both as a target and as a dubious haven when a shot-up engine forced them to make an emergency landing.

Back row from left: *Co-pilot* Herb Harter, *navigator* John Weller, *nose gunner* Victor Crowell, *radar operator* Dick David, *tail gunner* Doyle Ebel, and *engineer* Bob Larson; front row: *waist gunner* Ray Fritter, *bombardier* Greg Babykin, *pilot* Frank Jeter, *radio operator* Dale Henderson, and *ball turret gunner* Sam Tillery. *Photo courtesy of the Jeter Crew.*

Picture this: it's 1944 and 11 young men—more precisely described as boys—are sailing high above the depths of a vast war-torn ocean in a flying box car called a B-24 Liberator. Their job out of high school is to keep this unwieldy airship aloft. Keep it aloft despite all forces that would bring it down. Keep it aloft long and far enough to locate the enemy target, drop their bombs, avoid crippling blows and get hundreds of miles back to the presumed safety of a friendly cot in a tent on a tiny muddy island in the Pacific.

This World War II aircraft is not the war plane flyboys know today. This plane is not pressurized. That means our lads are exposed to open air at altitudes up to 20,000 feet. Pilot Frank Jeter, co-pilot Herb Harter, and navigator John Weller sit aboard a heated flight deck. The others wear flight suits that shield them from the below freezing temperatures. But they're by no means protected from the cruel elements in effect at these heights.

Vic Crowell, the nose gunner, and bombardier Greg Babykin are in the nose turret on the front end of the plane. Only a piece of Plexiglas shields them from enemy fire or collision. Sam Tillery, the ladies man and the tallest of the group, is crouched in the ball turret on the bottom of the plane. The turret has to be retracted before the landing gear can come down. But during combat, the turret—with Sammy firing from within it—juts out from the bottom of the craft.

In the middle of the plane are Ray Fritter, a man of faith and waist gunner; engineer Bob Larson; radio operator Dale Henderson, and radar operator Dick David. Texan Doyle Ebel is hanging out behind the rudders in the tail gunner position. From this position he can lean out the open window and see if the bombs hit their target.

In this particular B-24 bomber, the crew members behave as if they're not afraid. They act like teammates on a football team. This could be the homecoming game back at San Jose High School for navigator John Weller. John's job at 22 is to get his crew there — wherever the day's target might be. In 1944 there was no such thing as GPS (global positioning satellites) to guide the way. He had to do it the hard way.

Often, he asks his loyal teammate Dale Henderson, the radio operator, to hold onto his legs while he climbs up through the escape hatch on the flight deck to get a fix on the stars on a night mission. He uses a sextant to get three readings on celestial bodies for a directional heading for the pilot. He stays below the slip stream — the air rushing across the top of the plane — so he won't get pulled out of the plane by its force. John trusts Dale implicitly.

John also puts his faith in the rest of the crew to help him sight land when he believes he is within 50 miles of their destination. Small islands in a huge ocean are difficult to spot, so 11 pairs of eyes are all put to work as pilot Frank Jeter prepares to fly in a square search pattern if a land mass is not sighted at the estimated time of arrival (ETA). Wishing to avoid the fate of Amelia Earhart a decade earlier in the same arena, these flyboys fall into line, each realizing their fate rests with each other.

At 22, pilot Frank Jeter was loved and respected by his crew. When he was flying, no one ever questioned his skill, level of responsibility, integrity or judgment. By all accounts he was a great pilot and a collaborator who listened to others before making a decision, however big or small. But when he was away from the plane, he was always ready to party.

To drink alcohol seemed like a ritual to Frank. He wanted and expected members of the crew to drink with him. In fact, several crew members recalled that he wanted to see if they could hold their liquor before he confirmed their acceptance on his crew. Given the terror of the war situation, it's no wonder that these flyers needed an antidote to the stress. Indeed, the enlisted men were invited to drop by the air base dispensary after each bombing mission to collect a shot or two of whiskey to "calm their nerves."

So how were these boys different from the hundreds of B-24 air crewmen that flew above the Pacific during World War II? First off, they were luckier than about half of their peers — they survived. The statistics were grim, and this particular crew watched as other bombers went down. They lost friends whose missions had been identical to theirs. They couldn't think about the danger. They refused to believe they could become one of the disasters that were so routine in the Pacific Theater in 1943-1945.

Frank Jeter's crew also stands out as a team that figured out together how to beat the odds to survive a forced landing in the middle of a nighttime ground battle on Iwo Jima in March of 1945. With aviation know-how and teamwork they repaired their own warplane and lived to complete another 16 missions before the war ended.

In 1964, Elleston Trevor wrote a popular novel whose story line jogged the Jeter Crew members' memory of their own almost tragic end. Elleston's book, *The Flight of the Phoenix* (Harper & Row Publishers), resonated for the airmen who recalled dropping out of the sky into a danger zone and using their resourcefulness to get back in the air and eventually home to their families. "Even though the circumstances are different, the same thing happened to us and our story isn't fictional," John Weller related. Trevor's book was made into a film in 1965 that starred Jimmy Stewart and a remake in 2004 featuring Dennis Quaid.

The Jeter boys were good friends, like brothers, and remained as such long after the war, they will tell you. The officers — pilot Frank Jeter, navigator John Weller, bombardier Greg Babykin and co-pilot Herb Harter — didn't separate themselves from the enlisted members of the crew. Even though they didn't live together in the same tent, a separation dictated by the army, they were in one another's company constantly. They even managed to rig up a telephone line between the officers and the enlisted men's tents. They ate together, drank together and took R & R (rest and recreation) together. Unlike the officers, the enlisted men were not allowed to have hard liquor or more than five beers in their possession. Led by Jeter, the officers had no qualms about sharing their booze with the enlisted guys.

The Jeter Crew's war legacy looms large to this day due to two factors: the lifelong friendships that formed in the horror of war and the amazing films they managed to create, get past the censors, and preserve as a record of their time together. Equipped with pilot Jeter's own amateur movie camera, the crew members took turns documenting their daily lives and their missions.

They filmed one another getting their plane ready for a mission, taking their places in the B-24, views of the target and the dropping and landing of their bombs. They filmed each other having breakfast on the ground at Iwo Jima, replacing the engine of their disabled plane and in flight on a later mission to bomb Shanghai. They filmed a fellow B-24 bomber at the Jeter Crew's side on the way to Shanghai. It was a bomber called Night Mission, which was shot down—and all the crew lost—above a target a few weeks later.

Pilot Frank Jeter gladly posed in front of his beloved Jeeter Bug, the B-24 he spotted on an airfield and decided he wanted to fly. It was mere coincidence the plane had a moniker that implied it was named after his crew. Unknown to Jeter or any of the crew at the time, the Jeeter Bug would many years later add glamour and a catchy name to the telling of their atypical experiences over the Pacific.

The unearthing of the cans of film about 1980 led to a revival of wartime memories and a compelling desire to reunite the crew. The films, developed after the war, had been stashed in a closet at Frank Jeter's Dallas home. When radio man Dale Henderson learned of the film's existence, he went into high gear. He had them converted to VHS for the rest of the crew members.

A history teacher in Oregon schools, Henderson had a keen interest in the films and the revival of the Jeter Crew friendships. He pulled out his own log of all the crew's missions and recorded his recollection of each of the 37 missions. He also resurrected his 1943 journal in which he described his first impressions of his fellow aviators.

Henderson insisted that all members of the crew be contacted and that they show up at a Denver reunion of the 11th Bombardment

Group of which the 26th Bomb Squadron was a part. Eight of 11 crew members (missing engineer Larson, nose gunner Crowell and ball turret gunner Tillery) met in Denver in 1979 and agreed to continue to get together as often as possible.

Over the years, John Weller and Henderson worked together to compile more of the Jeter Crew's history. That included individual crew member accounts of particularly scary episodes in the air and a biography of each of the now retired men up to about the year 2000. Like most World War II survivors, these men came back to the U.S. and resumed their lives as college students, craftsmen, professionals or businessmen. For the most part, they would live what most would consider normal mid-20th century lives despite their role in the nightmare of world war.

In 2002, navigator Weller met retiring NBC photo journalist Charles Sullivan by chance at his health club in San Jose. Sullivan, a new member of the club, asked John for directions, and a conversation ensued. Sullivan was intrigued by the prospect of mining the World War II films that John told him about for a documentary. He made connections for John and ultimately "The Jeeter Bug" became a 2005 PBS film featuring the crew's movies and interviews with six of the crew members. All six men interviewed for the film attended the premiere in February of 2005. Sadly, after its airing on PBS bombardier Greg Babykin passed away.

The story in film and words illuminates the inner thoughts of these ordinary American boys who went to war in 1944. Little did they understand when they answered the call to duty that they would instinctively band together to overcome the 50-50 odds that they would never see home and family.

Frank Jeter picked the Jeeter Bug as his favorite B-24.

The Jeter Crew's first mission was flown aboard Salty Sal on November 28, 1944. *Photos courtesy of the Jeter Crew.*

Top photo,
Pilots Jack Iso,
left, and Frank
Jeter on Saipan.
At left, Iso with
his pet dog.
*Photos courtesy
of the Jeter
Crew.*

Top photo, buddies Jim Haigh, center, and John Weller, right, with friend on Saipan. At right, bombardier Ben Squibb and Weller; above, Weller. Haigh and Squibb were killed with pilot Jack Iso in a December 1944 crash. *Photos courtesy of the Jeter Crew.*

Doyle Ebel and Ray Fritter on Saipan. *Photos courtesy of the Jeter Crew.*

Keystone K-8 Model movie camera, used by Jeter Crew to film the war. *Keystone photo.*

Chester "Jim" Haigh, friend lost in B-24 crash December 27, 1944, with pilot Jack Iso.

Victor Crowell and Dale Henderson dig a foxhole on Saipan, 1944.

A pet dog was the center of attention here with "Mac" standing at left, Greg Babykin, on ground left, Jack Iso, foreground, Herb Harter, "Chubby" Brandon, Joe Watson, Jim Haigh and Frank Jeter. *Photos courtesy of the Jeter Crew.*

The Jeter Crew's first mission: Iwo Jima, November 28, 1944. *Photo from Dale Henderson collection.*

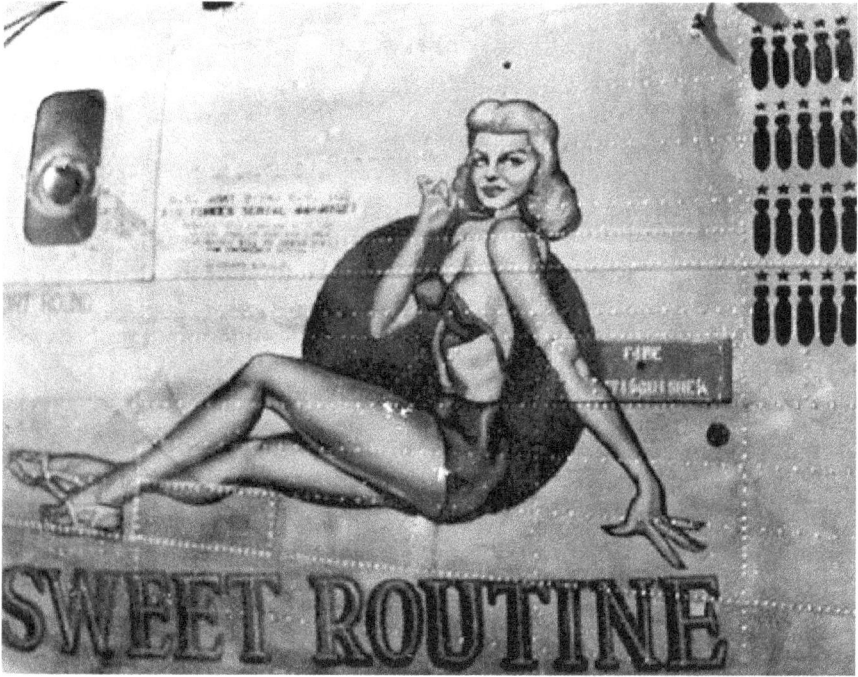

Frank Jeter's crew was flying Sweet Routine on the underpowered near-miss takeoff from Saipan on January 3, 1945. This is the B-24 Paul Farnham's crew crashed in on takeoff from Guam on June 26, 1945.

The cockpit of a B-24 bomber. *Photos courtesy of the Jeter Crew.*

Noon-time Japanese air raid on Saipan, November 27, 1944. A B-29 bomber is burning on the airstrip in the background. Three B-29s were destroyed in the Zeke attack, and fourteen enemy planes were shot down. Jeter Crew members surveying the damage from left to right: Ray Fritter, Doyle Ebel, Bob Larson, Victor Crowell, and Dale Henderson. *Photo courtesy of the Jeter Crew.*

Top photo, bombardier Greg Babykin with 500-pound bombs.
Above left, Ray Fritter and Doyle Ebel; at right, in front, Dale
Henderson and Fritter, standing, Vic Crowell and Bob Larson.
Photos courtesy of the Jeter Crew.

Dale Henderson and Ray Fritter move from a tent camp to a new Quonset hut on Saipan, early 1945. *Photo courtesy of the Jeter Crew.*

CHAPTER 2: GETTING TOGETHER AS A B-24 CREW

Some time shortly after the Japanese Pearl Harbor attack and President Roosevelt's declaration of war, each one of the Jeter Crew members woke up to the reality that they would probably be called to fight the war in some fashion. On this day of awakening, each boy had to reassess his life and put his ambitions—and his pleasures—aside to get this ugly global war out of their way. Every able-bodied young American male would inevitably serve in one way or another.

Before the Jeter Crew was even imagined, the individual members were taking steps to get ready for the experience of their lives. They all seemed to embrace the idea of defending America and quickly joined the Army. There were four Texans, pilot Frank Jeter, in Dallas supporting a family and running his late father's floor covering business; co-pilot Herb Harter who already knew how to pilot an aircraft; Victor Crowell, a high school student from a tiny oil town; and Doyle Ebel who was a mechanic. Two Californians, John Weller and Ray Fritter, were attending San Jose State College. A third Californian, Dale Henderson, was enrolled at a college in Los Angeles; Greg Babykin, from New York City, was a student at Duke University. Bob Larson was a South Dakota dust bowl farmer, Dick David, a Chicago banker, and Sam Tillery, a sheet metal worker from Arkansas.

Nine of the crew members met for the first time at Hammer Field in Fresno, California, in late March of 1944. Each one had received the necessary training to become part of an Army flight team. When they joined Frank Jeter's crew, these young men didn't have a clue what their future held or how close they would become to each other. They didn't have any idea that they would *have to* become a tight-knit crew whose members relied on each other for their very survival.

The Army brass set up many poles out in a field and each one was marked with a crew number. The officers—co-pilot Herb

Harter, navigator John Weller and bombardier Greg Babykin—were invited to join Frank Jeter at pole B-18. Then the enlisted men were assigned: Victor Crowell as nose gunner; Sam Tillery as the ball turret gunner; Bob Larson as flight engineer; Ray Fritter as waist gunner; and Doyle Ebel as tail gunner. On April 7, the air crews were transferred to March Field near San Bernardino in Southern California. Dale Henderson had been assigned to a different B-24 crew but was dropped as soon as he got to March Field. On April 11, Frank Jeter went to the barracks looking for a radio operator and asked Dale to join the crew. Dick David, who was already in the South Pacific, wouldn't join the crew as radar operator until January of 1945.

In the coming months, while the boys undertook their over-seas training at March Field, Jeter would test his crew in many ways. One test he put to each one of them was: can you hold your liquor?

Navigator John Weller described his first impression of Jeter's drinking. Weller: "He probably had to be the biggest swinger I'd seen in a long time." Weller describes the day he met Frank Jeter and was selected to be the crew navigator. "He was wearing sun-glasses, but it was obvious he was very hung over. He took me out to the bar and ordered a 'Zombie.' If you know what a Zombie is, you know how big it is and how much liquor's in it. Well, I drank it, and Frank said 'you're on my crew,'" Weller recalls with a chuckle.

Was being able to drink really a criterion for being accepted on Jeter's Crew? It's doubtful. In fact at least two of the crew—Bob Larson and Ray Fritter—didn't drink. Frank's attitude toward alcohol was emblematic of the type of carefree person he was on the ground, although all the crewmen profess that Frank Jeter took his role as flight commander quite seriously. He also put his full trust in each crew member once he knew the individual could competently perform his specialized task. The wives of the married crew members were allowed to stay with their husbands as the men trained at March Field. This arrangement allowed the Jeter Crew wives to begin a strong, life-long bond with the other crew members' spouses.

Meanwhile, another bonding was taking place at March Field. John Weller, Frank Jeter and Herb Harter became buddies with Jack Iso, a B-24 pilot from San Francisco, and his co-pilot Chester "Jim" Haigh, from Los Angeles. They bonded quickly, so much so that the Jeter boys attended Jack's wedding at the Riverside Mission Inn, which took place before their stay at March Field ended on June 22, 1944.

Jim's mother happened to be the governess for the two children of famed composer and music director Walter Scharf who was well connected in Hollywood. In the spring of 1944, Scharf was winding up production on the movie "Brazil," also called "Stars and Guitars," and invited the young men to visit the set. "The film starred Tito Guizar and Veloz and Yolanda (dancers)," John recalled. "I found it kinda amusing because Tito Guizar was walking along a sidewalk on the set, and the sidewalk was made out of wood and it squeaked, so they had to stop filming." The film also featured Roy Rogers and his horse Trigger playing themselves.

John also recalls meeting actress Alice Faye through Scharf's wife, Betty, who had danced with Faye when they were girls in New York in Rudy Valle's troupe. "Betty was a stand-in (actress) for Alice Faye. She looked quite a bit like Alice. She had the same coloring." Betty took the boys on a trip to Rodeo Drive where they met Alice who invited them to go shopping. "She said she was going to Adrien's, a very exclusive shop where they have women who model all the clothes. She said she wanted to buy some lingerie. We said we had to decline," he said with a laugh.

Walter Scharf invited Herb, John and Jim out to many places, and he would pick them up in his 12-cylinder Lincoln. "He was so well known that if we went to a show he wouldn't even have to say anything and they cleared out the loge section so we could sit there. The same thing would happen in a restaurant. We would always get the best table," John chuckles. It was very nice to get to meet some famous people, and they treated us so nice. They always introduced us as Army flyboys."

When Scharf wound up his work on "Brazil" he asked the

boys if they would like to come to the cast party. "He said: 'bring a date.' I told him being new to the area I didn't know anyone that I could bring. So he said: 'just pick out one of the Golden Girls (famous dancers at the time) and ask her if she'd like to go to the party with you.' So my country boy side comes out and I asked him: 'What if she has a husband or a boyfriend?' And he says: 'Look John I'm the director here' like she wouldn't say no. Anyway, we pulled a night flight on the day of the party so we didn't get to go anyway."

By the time the crews left March Field for overseas duty, Jack Iso and Jim Haigh had become good friends with several members of the Jeter Crew. The two crews were together again on Saipan with the 30th Bombardment Group in late 1944 so the Jeter boys had a chance to hang out with Iso's group when they weren't flying missions. Greg, Herb and Frank got to know more of the Iso Crew members, including bombardier Benjamin Squibb, who was also from Los Angeles.

The Jeter Crew stayed at March Field in sunny California for training for almost three months. Jeter took them out on test flights in the area before they left for duty overseas. On one particular flight, their B-24 lost its electrical system over the desert. Frank told everyone on the flight deck to put on their parachutes and asked John Weller to tell everyone in the back to get ready to jump. Hearing this scary admonition, Sam Tillery, the armorer, looked right into John's eyes and said: "Lt. you have to promise me that you'll be the last one out of the plane!" Luckily, no one had to jump because the plane suddenly got its power back. "Sam and I have talked about this many times. He still remembers it vividly," John said.

On June 23, 1944, the Jeter Crew went to Fort Lawton at Seattle, Washington, for debarkation. There they boarded a ship called the S.S. Shawnee, which took them across the Pacific Ocean to Oahu, Hawaii, and advanced training as replacements for the 7th Bomber Command and 7th Air Force. "After six miserable days wearing our winter uniforms on the ship, we arrived in the Hawaiian Islands. So the first thing was to buy some suntan uniforms and ship the winter duds home. We didn't need much in the way of clothes, only for dress occasions. Otherwise, it was shorts, swim trunks, T-shirts or no shirts, and lightweight coveralls as flight suits.

Assigned to Kahuku Army Air Base on the northern tip of Oahu, the Jeter Crew settled in for three more months of training to learn more about bombing and weapons and gain experience flying the B-24. For John Weller, key to his proficiency as the way finder was to learn over-water navigation. "In Europe, they had landmarks so they could use overland techniques, but in the Pacific it was a totally different story. In the short period of replacement training, I had no over-water or celestial navigation. So when we were assigned to the 7th Air Force replacement unit, I had to learn over-water navigation for both night and day long-distance flights."

Toward the end of their stay at Kahuku, the Jeter Crew was ready to fly a training mission on their own. "After three months of learning how to navigate over water, we had the opportunity to fly to a tiny Naval base called Palmyra," Weller related. "It's about six degrees above the equator and about 600 miles south of Oahu. The currents come in from both directions and make the island a great place for fish to propagate, including sharks and so forth."

"The Navy had taken Palmyra over, and all they were doing there was repairing small crafts, nothing big, nothing big at all. It was such a beautiful place! A photographer's utopia." The Jeter boys were enchanted by the beauty and calm of the idyllic location far from anything related to war in the vast Pacific. They were expected back in Hawaii the same day, but pilot Frank Jeter fudged a little and radioed back that they had some engine trouble and needed to stay overnight.

"We decided we didn't want to go back to Oahu right away. So we figured a way to stay and enjoy ourselves, and the Navy supplied us with all the libations we needed. Even the pilot was climbing trees to get the coconuts down. We had a great time, and went back the next morning," Weller related.

Today Palmyra remains one of the very few Pacific islands virtually untouched by war, tourism or industry. The Nature Conservancy purchased the tiny island in 2001 and maintains its pristine state, which allows the native sea and island creatures to thrive.

CHAPTER 3: SURVIVAL ON A WARTIME PACIFIC ISLAND

Growing up in America during the Great Depression, the Jeter Crew guys were accustomed to enduring hardship and shortages. But they could not have imagined how different their lives would become once they got to the Pacific war. Putting their lives in jeopardy in the skies above enemy territory, these flyboys could only dream about taking refuge in a soft, warm bed or indulging in one of Mom's home cooked meals. Instead, they came "home" to tents in places like Saipan where the Japanese were still dropping bombs and later to Guam and Okinawa where living conditions were far from ideal.

As children of a severely depressed economy, these boys accepted the difficulties as if the conditions were normal and often made light of problems in getting food and a comfortable place to rest their weary heads. "I think Doyle (Ebel) said it best: we started out with nothing so we were grateful for whatever we were given. We didn't complain too much," John Weller said.

Even though Army air crews didn't set up base on an island until after the Allies had taken it, danger still existed on the former Japanese islands. On Saipan, the Jeter Crew endured nine Japanese air strikes between November 27, 1944, and January 5, 1945. When the alarm went up, the crew members took to the foxholes and waited out the attack. They often drank until the raid was over.

On the first attack, just after midnight on November 27, one Japanese plane strafed the large Saipan runway and hit two gas trucks. One B-29 exploded killing three men; two other B-29s were damaged. The same day at noon, innumerable Zekes (Mitsubishi-made A6M Zeros, Japanese long-range fighters) strafed both runways destroying three B-29s. Fourteen Japanese planes were shot down. Sadly, a Navy tanker in a cove below Guam shot down a U.S. P-47. "Tough to see your own hit by friendly fire," Dale Henderson wrote in his log of the Saipan air raids.

Henderson wrote about a low level pass over the island by 10 Japanese Bettys (G4M, a land-based attack plane made by Mitsubishi). One of them flew right over the crew's tent. Six were shot down but not before they hit two B-29s, both complete losses. "Fox hole felt damn good," Henderson wrote. On Christmas night beginning at 8, 25 Bettys made four consecutive passes over the island. They destroyed one B-29 and damaged two others. "Heard falling bomb for the first time, sounded like plane on strafing attack. (Allied) night fighters got two planes, which we saw, and two others."

On the day after Christmas, the Jeter Crew was stuck in fox-holes for three hours. That night the Japanese hit B-29s on Tinian and killed 14 men on Saipan with a bomb that hit their hut. The attacks petered out by early January: on the 2nd at 3 in the morning two Japanese planes were shot down by night fighters, but not before they dropped three bombs, one that went off an hour later. On the 3rd, the boys saw one Japanese plane shot down, but none flew over Saipan. The last alarm sounded at 6 a.m. on January 5 but nothing happened. "It just got us up. The alert only lasted 10 minutes," Henderson's log concluded.

Danger on Saipan also took the form of "diehard" Japanese soldiers who had refused to surrender and taken refuge in the jungle. Knowledge of their presence kept the Jeter boys on edge, and they always kept their .45 pistols at their side. One night as the officers slept in their tent, wearing just their undershorts and with the tent flap up, they were disturbed by a strange visitor about 3 a.m. Greg suddenly felt something bump him from under his bed. He shifted around on the cot and moved his leg to one side. As he lowered his leg, he felt something warm and sweaty with bristles like rough and sharp hair.

John Weller recalled the hysterical moment: "Greg shouted, "It's a Jap! And he grabbed his .45 and jumped out of bed and started shooting. We all grabbed our .45s and ran out of the tent and started shooting too. Then we heard a strange and animalistic sound. It was like oink, oink, oink, and we figured out it was a couple of wild pigs come to root!" Although, the guys found it funny and laughed about it, they soon realized what a dangerous situation they had just experienced. "We could have killed someone," Weller said. "We were lucky."

Although the airmen seemed to overact to the pig invasion, the possibility of desperate Japanese soldiers showing up at their tent in the wee hours of the morning was a real worry. The Allies were aware that an undetermined number of Japanese hold-outs were still around the defeated islands hoping for the opportunity to kill some Americans. [1]

A series of beer thefts from a refrigerator in a makeshift club house on Saipan left the Jeter boys wondering. Each crew member was allotted six bottles of beer a week when it was available on the island. The airmen had tried to take advantage of the cooling effects of flight altitude by taking the tepid beer up on missions. But that practice didn't work very well because by the time they got back to camp, the beer was warm again. So they managed to get a small refrigerator where they stored the bottles until they were ready to imbibe.

"We put our names on the beer, and we knew it wasn't our guys stealing from us," recalled Weller. We suspected it was Japanese soldiers who came out of hiding at night. As the bottles continued to disappear, the crew members devised a plan to halt the thefts. "I know it sounds terrible, but what we did was urinate in a couple of beer bottles. We put the caps back on and put them in the refrigerator. We never had any more beer disappear after that."

You might think that Uncle Sam's fighting boys would have plenty to eat to maintain their strength and energy to successfully accomplish their bombing missions. Not so. Food was hard to come by for these Army Air Corps combatants. The U.S. Navy, however, seemed to have plenty, so the Jeter Crew had to develop prodigious scrounging skills to score nourishing food, such as steak.

---

1   In 1972, local hunters discovered a diehard Japanese soldier living in a cave on Guam, 27 years after the war was over. He was rescued and brought back to Tokyo where it took a while to convince him the war was over. Source: Mike Lanchin, BBC World Service, BBC News Magazine, January 23, 2012

Before taking off on a mission, the crew members would have coffee, one thin pancake covered with watery green-colored sugar for syrup, and powdered eggs, all terrible, John recalled. On a 10-12 hour bombing flight, they shared a can of turkey, a loaf of bread and a canteen of water. Regular mess food was powdered eggs, dehydrated potatoes, canned peaches and peas. Existing on this type of diet, the Jeter Crew members each lost 30 pounds or more during their combat duty.

One quest for sustenance that got the boys in a bit of trouble happened on Guam. It seems Doyle and Dale were the instigators and they talked Dick David into staging a night-time raid of a heavily laden banana tree that hung over a nearby officers' tent. Their mission to harvest a generous crop of the native fruit was successful but could have been disastrous.

Dick David tells the story: "We'd been eyeing the tree for a while. On Guam there had been banana and coconut plantations before the war and the trees were still growing there in our camp. So, one night before we were going out on a mission "Ebie" (Doyle Ebel) said, 'let's get some bananas to eat on the flight. Tonight's the night!'

"Ebie put me on his shoulders and I took a whack at the tree with an axe right above the tent. Well, I had the axe the wrong way around so nothing happened. The next time, I knocked the whole top of the tree off and it landed on the tent. I'm running, Ebie's running and they are firing at us. They thought we were Japs!"

Trading liquor or beer to sailors for food was not uncommon for the crew's scroungers. And they befriended the Seabees (Naval Construction Battalions)[2] by taking them on test flights

---

2   Rear Admiral Ben Moreell determined to activate, organize, and man Navy construction units. On 28 December 1941, he requested specific authority to carry out this decision, and on 5 January 1942, he gained authority from the Bureau of Navigation to recruit men from the construction trades for assignment to a Naval Construction Regiment composed of three Naval Construction Battalions.

of their newly repaired B-24 engines. In exchange, the Seabees invited them to get at the end of their mess line. Sometimes, though, their methods were a bit more extreme, like the time they absconded with a supply of rations recently unloaded from a Navy ship.

Weller explained: "We knew there were better rations being shipped in so we had to find a way to get them. Some of our scroungers found out that a load of "10-in-1" rations was sitting on the dock. A "10-in-1" case contained breakfast, lunch and dinner for 10 men. Breakfast was canned eggs with bacon or ham, dry biscuits and some canned fruit. The balance of canned meat, cheese, and a very concentrated chocolate bar completed a day's meal.

"Our scroungers contacted our flight surgeon and asked him if they could borrow an ambulance. He wanted to know why. After finding out what was up, he said: 'Sure, but I want two cases for myself!' The scroungers went sirens blaring down to the docks. They had a story to tell the men in charge. The story was that there were lots of wounded back at base that needed food. It worked!"

The Army airmen in the Pacific Theater only got fresh meat about once a month, so whenever they could they used their wits to acquire a meal of turkey or beef from the Navy stores. One day towards the end of the war the Jeter boys found themselves with an adequate supply of liquor, but no food. "One of our crew

---

2 CONTINUED. During the Second World War, the Seabees performed in both the Atlantic and Pacific Theaters of Operation. At a cost of nearly $11 billion and many casualties, they constructed over 400 advanced bases along five figurative "roads" which all had their beginnings in the continental United States. The South Atlantic road wound through the Caribbean Sea to Africa, Sicily, and up the Italian peninsula. The North Atlantic road passed through Newfoundland to Iceland, Great Britain, France, and Germany. The North Pacific road passed through Alaska and along the Aleutian Island chain. The Central Pacific road passed through the Hawaiian, Marshall, Gilbert, Mariana, and Ryukyu Islands. The South Pacific road went through the South Sea islands to Samoa, the Solomons, New Guinea, and the Philippines. All the Pacific roads converged on Japan and the Asiatic mainland. Source: Wikipedia

knew the mess sergeant for the commanding officer (CO) and asked him if he would like a few drinks. He said yes. The catch was he had to bring a roast turkey basted in butter to the party. We knew the CO had food. He (the mess sergeant) agreed and arrived with the turkey.

"After the party, he invited us back to the CO's mess for steak," Weller continued. "The CO never missed the turkey or the steak. We were pretty hardened by this time and didn't care (if the food was missed). We knew they needed us. Replacements were not readily available."

Not only was the food scarce but the climate and general environment of a tropical island could be challenging. The weather was hot and humid year-round; bugs such as mosquitoes, flies and cockroaches were abundant; and rats abounded. John Weller remembers feeling a rat scampering up his arm while he slept. Today he isn't sure whether it really happened or if it was just a bad dream. The men sprayed themselves with DDT, an insecticide now banned in the U.S., and placed empty tin cans under each leg of their cots to keep small rodents from crawling into bed with them.

Rain was constant during the wet season from July to November, leaving the ground as one big mud hole and making it difficult to walk around and to maneuver equipment. By default, the Army Air Corps dress code hardly applied, and the Jeter boys generally wore shorts or swim trunks with T-shirts or no shirts when they weren't flying.

They slept in tents with crushed coral floors and kept a flap up to allow the light winds to cool them down a bit in their beds. On Guam they had an indoor latrine, showers, and a laundry. A place to wash sticky, sweaty clothes in such a climate was considered by some to be a must. Although in a forward area, the Jeter boys could at least enjoy the luxury of electrical power in their tents so they could have light to read by and radios to listen to the limited programs available. They could tune in to "Tokyo Rose," who taunted them with tales of unfaithful women and Japanese intrigue. When they weren't on a mission, the airmen on Guam could enjoy a Hollywood movie just about every night, courtesy of the U.S. Navy.

Amidst the rigors of war, the Jeter boys often found ways to enjoy themselves. One example is the dances they arranged with the nurses who worked at the Army hospital on Saipan. "We found some Samoans who had some of their native (musical) instruments," recalled John Weller. "Between missions, we would go to the hospital and see if any of the nurses would come and dance with us.

"We'd get a Quonset hut and get a native band to play and invite the nurses—who were working their butts off… They were wonderful ladies who were working long shifts to take care of the wounded. Still two or three would take time to come dance with us. Their rule was to dance one dance with each man. There were 30 or so of us—this was many dances for them. I recall they took off their army issue shoes."

By pure coincidence, John encountered one of the nurses 50 years later in San Jose, California, where he was volunteering to help senior citizens with their taxes. She told him she had been an Army nurse on Saipan during World War II. "I asked her: 'Do you remember a bunch of flyboys coming up to the hospital and inviting you to come dance with us?' She said she did and I said: 'Thank you for the dance.' After all these years, I was grateful for the opportunity to thank her personally."

The Jeter boys often had plenty of beer or liquor to fuel a raucous party. One night on Okinawa, the crew got a windfall of two quarts each of Old Overholt rye whiskey. They had already planned to have a party that night in the officers' tent, and the whiskey gave a new dimension to the celebration. After they'd had a few drinks, all but three of them dropped out of the action: "Victor Crowell was a young fella and all you had to do was pass a cork in front of him and he was done, he was drunk," Doyle Ebel recalled.

John Weller became very tipsy and needed Doyle's help to get to the latrine on the other side of a small ditch they'd dug to keep rain water from flooding the tent. A few minutes later back in the tent, he went down. He'd had enough and was calling for the flight surgeon (the squadron doctor). "He *swore* he was gonna die. He swore he was *dying*," Doyle recalled. John explained years later that he was worried about the combined effect of the whiskey and a Benzedrine nasal spray he had taken for a cold. "So we got the flight surgeon to come and check him. The doctor said he was fine and assured him he wasn't gonna die that night. Then he passed out."

So there were only three left at the party: Frank Jeter, Sam Tillery and Doyle Ebel. "About 3 a.m., I was really feeling no pain, and I looked at Sam and said, 'I've had enough. I got to go.' Sam said, 'Me too,' and we started out of the tent," Doyle remembered. "Frank, who was a professional drinker—we all graduated from the Jeter School of Drinking—called after us: 'Party poopers!'

"Well, it was raining that night, like a constant drizzle," he continued. "It rained just about every night there." So the boys had to trudge through thick, red clay mud to get back to their tent, which was uphill from the officers' tent. They had to cross an elevated narrow gauge railroad track that had been used before the war to haul cane to the island sugar mill. The track was at the top of a 10-foot red clay embankment that was soaked with rain.

"Sam and I started up the hill and we just kept sliding back to the bottom. We did that about four times. We were two drunks trying to get over a slippery hill," he recalled. Lying at the bottom of the hill in the mud, Doyle and Sam got the idea of taking a different nearby route, using a patch of weeds for traction. It worked and they climbed over to the other side. When they got to their tent, Doyle and Sam collapsed onto their canvas cots and fell fast asleep without changing out of their cut-off khaki shorts.

Doyle's telling of the story of the day after: "The next morning some friends of mine from another crew came to wake me up. They said, 'Get up! There's going to be a big dinner. This was about 10 or 11. When I started to get up, I couldn't move, and I said, 'I can't get up.' They were just standing there laughing at me, and I said 'Hey fellas, this is serious. I'm paralyzed!' I was getting real perturbed because I was *paralyzed* and they were *laughing*. I was really worried 'cause we had been warned not to drink home-made booze over there because you could become paralyzed or go blind or something. I was thinking, 'I didn't drink anything bad, just what the doc had given me.' "

Momentarily, Doyle realized that his whole body was covered with a thick layer of dried red clay mud. "It was like being in a full body cast." At that point his buddies helped him into the shower and he rinsed off the mud and regained his mobility. Sam, who suffered a similar phenomenon, was less dramatic and took himself for a good wash before dinner.

Co-pilot Herb Harter and bombardier Greg Babykin, accustomed to their battle being with the Japanese, found themselves in mortal danger combating nature one day of leisure on Saipan. Herb tells the story in his own words:

"Strangely enough, my most frightening and dangerous wartime experience did not involve flying. While stationed on Saipan, Greg Babykin and I had a day off. From our tent, we could see the beautiful, blue ocean out beyond the vegetation and rocks that covered the island, so we decided to explore. With some make-shift fishing gear, food, and a trusty carbine, we headed out.

"After a long hike, we neared the edge of the island and discovered a very steep trail leading down to the ocean. It was flanked on either side by sheer cliffs, 100 feet or more high. At the bottom of the trail, we found no beach, but rather a long, narrow ledge cut along the side of the island. At the back of the ledge was a shallow cave cut into the rock.

"The ledge itself, covered with tide pools, coral and sea life, ended in a sheer cliff that dropped off into the Pacific. Peering over the ledge, we saw waves gently rising up the face of the rock to about five feet below us, and then gently dropping 30 feet or more as they rolled back out. It was a gentle deep blue ocean and beautiful sight.

"We proceeded along the ledge, picking our way over the rough surface. After a good stroll we found a peaceful, scenic spot where we sat down for a picnic. Then, looking out across the ocean, surrounded by spectacular natural beauty, I said, "Greg, I think I see a wave that's a little bigger than the others."

"Before we knew it, the peaceful blue water rose up and came crashing over the ledge, and all hell broke loose. Everything was picked up by the powerful wave and smashed against the little cave, including us! Then the churning whitewater reversed course and began to wash our lunch, fishing gear, rifle—and us—off the ledge.

"As we were dragged toward the ocean, we frantically tried to find a handhold on the rough stone, or the sharp coral, desperate to keep from being dragged over the 30-foot drop by the powerful wave. We knew if we went over the edge, we'd never be heard from again.

"As the wave dissipated, we scrambled to our feet, hands cut and bloody, and ran for our lives. Before we could reach the path, two more waves smashed into the cliff leaving us once again flattened on the ledge and holding on for dear life.

"After the war and until Greg passed away (in 2009), we talked on the telephone almost every month. Many times we mentioned the Saipan fishing trip, acknowledging how stupid it was to be lured down a path that had taken the ocean thousands of years to cut out of rock, and how lucky we both were to have lived through it. We often wondered how our disappearance would have been explained to our families since no one knew where we were and all the evidence went over the cliff."

CHAPTER 4: WE WILL COME HOME

U.S. Army training indoctrinated World War II aviators with a belief that they would prevail in whatever enemy threats they faced. By the time the Jeter Crew got to the Pacific war, they were convinced they would not become casualties. They would survive. In late 1944, as the crew went into the horrible Pacific island battles that claimed thousands of lives, they believed tragedy would strike others, not them.

From the first flight into the battle zone to the last cancelled mission scheduled for the day the war ended, these guys were in grave danger. Adrenaline and comradeship kept them going for the duration, despite troubles that cause them to shake even today when they recall them. Navigator John Weller, radio operator Dale Henderson, and tail gunner Doyle Ebel tell their stories of the tragedies that were averted, in some cases, just barely.

Throughout their eight months in the Pacific battle zone, twice crew members came close to falling out of the plane through an open bomb bay, and another time one of their engines conked out on takeoff almost sending them and their bombs into a hospital. They participated as decoys in a fighter mission over Truk, and they earned the Distinguished Flying Cross for a pre-invasion low-altitude strafing mission over Iwo Jima. They experienced a high speed stall that could easily have become a fatal crash.

These boys had the harrowing experience of being hit by anti-aircraft fire over a Japanese target, losing two engines and being forced to make an emergency landing in the middle of an Iwo Jima fire fight. One crew member was severely burned in a runway accident that killed 23 others, and they witnessed their fellow aviators crash into the Pacific Ocean, a fate that might be theirs.

On their November 17-18, 1944, flight from Oahu to Kwajalein to Saipan—on their way to their first combat station—the crew had a little bad luck when a huge squall enveloped them unexpectedly. Pilot Frank Jeter had to take the plane to a lower altitude to get out of the turbulence. With a change in altitude, navigator John's heading was no longer valid. He recalculated their position and when they neared the destination, everyone got involved in watching for land. Once Doyle spotted the island, everyone breathed again, and the smart ass tail gunner got on the intercom with the comment: "Lieutenant, you're off your ETA by five minutes." Both men still get a kick out of telling the story 66 years later, each with a slightly different version. Doyle remembers the ETA being off three minutes; John says five.

After the B-24 crew landed safely on Saipan where they would stage their first 19 missions, Frank took John aside. He said he would never question John's ability to expertly navigate. He would always leave John alone to do his job. His trust in John was solid. John soon came to understand that Frank relied on each crew member to function as an essential part of a well-oiled machine. He trusted them to keep their B-24 aloft, on course, and successful in its missions — as long as their luck held out.

On December 5, 1944, radioman Dale Henderson learned a valuable lesson about keeping in close touch with his air crew mates in flight. On the Jeter boys' second combat mission, they joined two other B-24s to bomb Pagan Island in a daylight raid. Henderson writes: "Our second mission was a milk run to Pagan, but it was almost my last. As we approached the target we were climbing and were at about 8,000 feet. I left my radio station to go back to my left waist gun position. I had my parachute in one hand and my chest chute in the other. As I reached the mid-point on the catwalk through the bomb bay, the bombardier tested the bomb bay doors. There I stood, chute in one hand, harness in the other, trying to figure out how I could put them on if I fell out. After what seemed like an eternity, the doors closed. From then on, the bombardier always knew when I was going to the rear."

For that mission, Henderson wrote on the mission log: "Milk run (aviation term for relatively safe mission). Only three plane raid. No flak or fighters. Bombs away 10:05. Combat time, 2:50; total combat time, 11 hours."

On December 17, the Jeter Crew flew the B-24 Pacific Passion on one of their group's first radar attacks — bombing a fogged-in island — but the craft had no radar equipment. To try to hone in on the target on Iwo Jima, navigator Weller used a stop watch and altitude table. "It was pretty crude," Weller said. "The flak was bad. I don't know if we hit our target." Henderson's log entry noted that one Zeke showed up during the 72 minutes they were over Iwo Jima, but he wasn't aggressive."

The Jeter Crew's collective belief that they were invincible was seriously challenged a few weeks later just after Christmas. Their good buddies on Jack Iso's B-24 crew, who put their faith in their lucky mascot, Minnie the Mongoose, suddenly seemed to be jinxed. Minnie, a motherless baby adopted by the crew in Honolulu months before, had withstood many flights with Iso's group despite an initial intolerance to the high altitudes. Iso's B-24 crew, who called their plane the Flying Mongoose, had been successful so far in its missions and had avoided getting hit despite heavy anti-aircraft activity over its targets. The crew, including Iso, Jim Haigh and Benjamin Squibb, were convinced the tiny creature was the St. Christopher's Medal that kept them flying safe. So when she was run over by a jeep on Christmas Eve, the airmen were shaken. Could Iso's crew continue their lucky streak or would it end with Minnie's demise?

Their first flight after her death didn't renew their confidence. Their plane blew an engine on the runway and hadn't been able to take flight. The next mission was aborted due to electrical problems. But on their third mission on December 27, 1944, it looked like they would make it. But it wasn't to be. They successfully dropped their bombs on their target and started back to Saipan. On the long trip home, their four engines failed one by one and their plane crashed into the sea. The bodies of pilot Iso, co-pilot Haigh and bombardier Squibb were never found; the other members of the crew were picked up by a rescue team and survived. On that mission, they were flying in Puddle Jumper II, a substitute for the Flying Mongoose.

On January 14, 1945, the Jeter Crew played the role of decoy in a joint raid to Truk with a P-38 fighter unit. Three B-24s flew at 10,000 feet, while the P-38s flew at 18,000 with clouds shielding the fighters from the Japanese's view. Henderson writes in the log: "Enemy thought we were sitting ducks. As they took off, we radioed and the P-38s got most while still on the runway. Several did make it, but not for long. At 9 o'clock a Zeke (Japanese long-range fighter) made it to about 7,000 feet. A P-38 came down, missed the climbing Zeke, did a complete loop, hung on his props and blasted away. The Zeke exploded. They got another, we saw a parachute."

This mission was written up in a military publication as one of the longest fighter missions in the Pacific war. The Jeter Crew and the fighters had flown 1,400 miles from Guam to Truk and back. Henderson concluded his log entry: Easy mission, no flak. We navigated P-38s back to Guam. One chick lost an engine and he tucked right under our wing. Great joint effort. No bombs." Truk had been the base for Japanese operations against Allied forces in New Guinea and the Solomon Islands. The island was heavily fortified and was known as the "Gibraltar of the Pacific."

Ten days later, Henderson's log entry would show more worry. On January 27, 1945, the Jeter Crew continued a string of bombing missions on Iwo Jima that started in November. Of this mission Henderson wrote: "Roughest yet, day mission, plenty of accurate flak. Hit the lead plane, (piloted by Herbert O.) Broemer right through the cockpit. Co-pilot and navigator severely wounded, also Broemer's right arm. After recovery he brought plane back with one arm. Socked in around island, like a hole in a doughnut, Iwo clear as a bell. Small ship by island. Into clouds after bombs away. Broemer out of control, almost hit us. We got one flak hole in top turret, missed Larson by two inches. Bombs hit target, some hit ship. We brought Broemer home, helped guide to landing."

The next mission to Iwo Jima on February 1 was also scary. It was a night mission and the Japanese spotted the Jeter Crew plane and threw up seven searchlights. Henderson wrote in the log: Ray and Dale throwing out radar window (chaff to jam Jap radar) like mad. Frank kept calling for more. Bucked headwind to target."

On February 15, 1945, just four days before the invasion of Iwo Jima, the Jeter Crew flew a day mission from Saipan to Iwo Jima. Henderson reported a successful mission with wide open target and no flak. However, he noted another crew spotting bombs was jumped by three enemy fighters. Coming back to Saipan the visibility was nil causing problems on landing. "A real sweat job, had to hit the deck," Henderson wrote.

On February 17, just two days before the marine invasion of Iwo Jima, the Jeter Crew participated in what Henderson called "The Big One." He wrote of the mission: "First pre-invasion raid. Went in at 500-1,000 feet. Right over (Mount) Suribachi, strafed all the way in. Laid 250 lb. radio fused frag bombs over trenches on beach. Great bombing. Battleships Texas and New Mexico shelling all the time. Not much flak (for us), or for the 38th, but 27th (Bomb Squadrons, also part of 30th Bomb Group) caught hell. Forty-three planes on mission." The Jeter Crew received the Distinguished Flying Cross for this mission.

On the actual Iwo Jima D-Day, February 19, the Jeter Crew was scheduled for a bomb mission but was called off by the Navy. Their Iwo Jima campaign was over and they were reassigned to the 26th Bomb Squadron of the 11th Bombardment Group, triggering a move to Guam. Ironically, about one month later the Jeter Crew would make an emergency landing during a fire fight on Iwo Jima in the same area they had dropped bombs from November 1944 to mid-February 1945.

You don't have to search too far to find records of a plethora of B-24 crashes in the proximity of the Jeter Crew's battleground — on Saipan, Guam and Okinawa — in the last six months of the Pacific War. That's not counting the crashing of many, many B-29s on ill-fated missions to bomb Japanese cities in the spring of 1945. Scores of planes dropped out of the sky for one reason or another: Hundreds of airmen either bailed out of crash-bound B-24s and risked being captured by the Japanese, or tried to make a water landing and hoped to survive and be rescued before the enemy found them. Some aircraft exploded and burned after being hit over their target, some lost engines due to flak or Japanese fighter hits, and some war-weary B-24s with mechanical problems that couldn't be properly repaired simply gave up the ghost. And of course, the infamous Japanese kamikaze pilots were also menacing the embattled airspace above their home islands.[3]

With the Iso crash still fresh and just weeks before the Jeter Boys joined their new squadron on Guam, two B-24 crews of the 26th Bomb Squad met their sad fate at the hands of the Japanese.

The first crew, led by pilot 1st Lt. Herman L. Bierwirth, was lost after their B-24 was rammed by a kamikaze pilot on their February 8 mission to Iwo Jima. The Zeke sneaked up on the formation of 10 planes that had just dropped their bombs and were about 10 miles east of the target. Eye witnesses said they caught a quick glimpse of the Zeke as it suddenly dived out of the low sun's blinding rays. They said the fighter with red roundels on the wings rolled, belly over and smashed into Bierwirth's top turret. The right wing broke off at the fuselage and both planes exploded. The heat from the explosion was felt by the men in the waist of the plane on Bierwirth's right wing. The wreckage flew apart and debris crashed in spectacular display into the sea 15,000 feet below. All 11 crew members perished.

Killed in the February 8 crash were: pilot Bierwirth, co-pilot Ralph B. Albaugh, navigator Fiume C. Cascioli, bombardier Harris G. Cheney, engineer Napoleon A. McMullen, radio operator Charles M. Finnigan, radar operator Donald E. Bloedel, assistant engineer Charles L. Conrad, armorer/gunner Johnnie Markham,

---

3 Long after the war, John Weller met a Japanese-American who had been conscripted for the Japanese Air Force even though he was an American citizen born in Watsonville, California. The fighter pilot had lost his mother when he was just 11, and his father had sent him and his siblings to Japan to live with relatives.

While chatting at a Rotary Club meeting, the two veterans figured out that they might have been in the same place at the same time. "We looked at each other and realized that we might have faced each other in battle over the Pacific. One of us could have shot the other one down," John said. "He said the military had him scheduled to become a Kamikaze pilot. He wanted no part of this so he got a medical deferment."

armorer/gunner Richard E. Carton, and radar operator John B. Van Volkenburg.

Two days later, another 26th Bomb Squad crew proved that no matter how celebrated a pilot was, nobody was invincible. Lt. Edwin Brashear had earned his share of glory. Flying the B-24 Hit Parade, Brashear had been credited with putting a Japanese destroyer out of commission in the harbor at Chi Chi Jima. His hometown newspaper in Texas carried an article about another of Brashear's displays of bravery and success:

"Around a sheer-faced cliff off tiny Kita Island in the Bonins, a formation of 7th Army Air Force Liberators (B-24s) roared, 50 feet above the water, to blast one large Japanese boat and strafe two others. The Liberators came in low to escape detection and, with a wing tip barely missing the 1,000 foot cliff, caught the large enemy boat by surprise and bombed it out of the water. The huge plane then continued on course and strafed the smaller companion boats.

"As the Hit Parade finished its strafing run, two Jap Zeros came in at the same altitude. But the 7th AAF Liberator resorted to evasive action and the enemy aircraft dived under, and pulled out at water level to resume the attack." Here 21-year-old Brashear is quoted: "After leveling off they headed upstairs. Soon they made a second pass, coming in from overhead.

"They fired at our nose and came in with full power," he told the newspaper. "One of them dropped a phosphorus bomb but his aim was off and we weren't hit. About that time one of the gunners in our formation fired a burst, and as his shells poured in to the cockpit, the fighter's canopy was shot off. With one Japanese fighter damaged, the two-plane interception stopped, and Lt. Brashear and his crew continued on their mission to bomb ground installations at Ha Ha Jima."

But Brashear's subsequent trip to Ha Ha Jima, his 30th mission, would not end so triumphantly, even though it was expected to be a milk run. Major Robert Holland had arranged the flight to Ha Ha Jima just after he returned to Guam from rest leave. Holland was a passenger in the lead plane, Royal Flush, piloted by Brashear on the February 10 mission.

Harry Gibbons was co-pilot with Harry McCallam's crew over Ha Ha Jima on the fated mission. Gibbons, who had flown on many missions in formation with Brashear's plane, wrote about Brashear's crash on the Pacific Wrecks Web site long after the war: "Brashear was generally the lead plane. He was good," Gibbons began.

"(Major Robert) Holland picked Ha Ha Jima, a couple of hundred miles north of Iwo. Therefore, we needed monstrous rubber tanks for gasoline carried in the bomb bays. If we were Laurel and Hardy we couldn't have fouled up the mission any worse. We flew from the west about 15,600 feet up. We had a tail wind. We always flew at 165 miles per hour. However, at that altitude with a strong wind behind us, we were probably doing close to 400 mph.

"After flying in view of the island for possibly five minutes, the Japs had good time to figure our altitude. It was when we released the bombs that his (Brashear's) plane took a hit in the bomb bay. Remember the gas-filled auxiliary tanks? It was an inferno. Brashear's plane (Royal Flush) turned out of control and headed back into the formation. From the distance it seemed two or three flyers got out. The tail gunner was rescued. The others had to be the waist window gunners. No one could have gotten out of the cabin.

"What a tragedy! Here was a crew that had shown enough leadership to be a lead crew and then have the ship taken over by an 'I'll show you guys how to fly guy.' . . . It's sick." Gibbons also shared his secret diary entry for the day: "Dangerous Critter, Ha Ha Jima, February 10. Another rough one. I feel a little uneasy. No appetite. Stomach upset a little. We were supposed to have an easy mission today but the lead ship picked up some ack ack (flak) in the bomb bay tank and caught fire right after bombs away. It was just a flying torch. A few fellows got out but some of them didn't have chutes on. That is two ships in two missions. Not so good. I had some friends on it too. I sweated this mission out but good, and then to see that plane peel off in front of us aflame sure put the finishing touches to it. I sometimes wonder if we'll ever get home. These extra missions are sure rough."

Killed on the flight were all but one crew member. The tail gunner, Staff Sgt. Richard E. Chandler, bailed out and was picked up three miles from Ha Ha Jima. Everyone else was killed including navigator 2nd Lt. Frank Curley from Philadelphia who, like the Jeter Crew's Ray Fritter, had plans to become a Catholic priest after the war. The others who perished were: co-pilot Theodore Robinson, bombardier Albert C. Reynolds, engineer William F. Caldwell, assistant engineer James T. McGee, radio operator Vincent Foti, radar operator Cecil K. Decker, armorer/gunner John J. Kerezsi, and Major Holland, classified as a passenger.

CHAPTER 5: IWO JIMA EMERGENCY LANDING

Frank Jeter's B-24 crew had been to Chi Chi Jima twice before. The tiny island was usually shrouded in a dense fog that kept bomb crews from seeing their target, but their radar could hone the bombs in precisely on the bulls-eye. The first time the Jeter Crew had bombed Chi Chi Jima was on Christmas Eve 1944. That day they had flown early, reaching Chi Chi about noon and getting home to Saipan by 3 p.m. Who wants to be on a bombing mission when it's almost Christmas, even in war?

Radio man Dale Henderson wrote in the log: "Easy mission, long trip. Target less than 500 miles from Tokyo. Island socked in, radar bombing, 11 flak bursts. Bombs away: 12:10. Combat time: 9:50 hrs.

The December 24th mission stood out as unusual among the more common Iwo Jima strikes made by the Jeter Crew during this time frame. Starting combat duty on Saipan on November 28, 1944, this group bombed Iwo Jima at least once a week until February 19, 1945, when the U.S. Marines invaded the island with the U.S. Navy attacking the Japanese battlements from off shore. After the ground battle began on Iwo Jima, the Jeter Crew was transferred to the 26th bomb squadron of the 11th Bombardment Group and moved to Guam. By that time, the Jeter boys had flown 19 bombing missions, 17 to Iwo Jima, and had racked up 169 hours of combat time.

Back in December and January, three Iwo Jima missions had been pretty treacherous. Henderson recorded the near miss of the December 12 outing: "Hot one. About the only plane not hit by flak. Red Zeke, 12 o'clock, attacked before target. Silver Zeke at nine, not aggressive. Green Tojo came out of the sun, came within 150 yards of tail. On December 30, Henderson logged another disaster averted: "Roughest flying weather encountered. Pea soup over target from 6,000 to 25,000 ft. Couldn't see wing tips, one mistake by a pilot and several planes could have gone down. Radar bombing. No flak, nor fighters." Another scary one: On January, 5, 1945, the Jeter Crew flew its first night snooper mission. When Greg Babykin, the bombardier, salvoed (released) the fragmentation bombs, one exploded under the plane. Henderson recorded: "Explosion spotlighted us, but searchlights didn't find us."

After the move to Guam, the Jeter Crew's first mission was to Chi Chi Jima, north of Iwo Jima in the Volcano Island group. Bombing missions there were meant to keep the airfields nonfunctional and to prohibit use of the harbor, which was a major communication base for the Japanese. On this day, March 3, 1945, again the island was hidden due to thick fog; this time the overcast reached up to 19,000. Hitting the target was no problem, however, because the radar worked so well. On March 11, the crew embarked on a day mission to Truk, another heavily fortified Japanese base, but they aborted due to an engine failure.

Although the crew members were still just barely old enough to be called men, they felt a certain bravado that kept their fear in check. By now, operating their unwieldy, yet fast and efficient flying machine was a job they felt confident about performing. By March 1945, these boys had flown over targets where their Japanese adversaries had opportunities to knock them out of the sky many times. They had dodged flak so far but it began to look like the odds were no longer in their favor.

On March 12, 1945, all of the crew's experience, knowledge, comradeship—and faith in each other—would be tested. The trip to Chi Chi Jima started out as a routine mission. The plane they flew that day was a loaner because their pilot's preferred ship, the Jeeter Bug, was in for maintenance. Little did these ordinary, yet brave, veritable whippersnappers know that this night mission—21st of their 37 sorties—would turn into a nightmare. They might have intuitively known though, that whatever kind of trouble they encountered over the big dark scary sea, their tight team would bring about a satisfying ending, thus proving the Jeter Crew was indeed one of the lucky ones.

Pilot Frank Jeter and his crew took off from Guam at 9:30 p.m. on March 12 with two extra rubberized gas tanks stashed in the bomb bay. The trip was a long one, about 1,000 miles, and the supplemental fuel was required to make the extra distance. Navigator John Weller found the way to Chi Chi Jima by consulting the stars. This was the Jeter Crew's third mission to Chi Chi but the first night snooper to this destination. Weller enlisted radio man Dale Henderson to hold onto his legs as he straddled two tables to take celestial fixes through the open escape hatch on the flight deck. "Believe me, this was trust," said Weller. "And laughingly, Dale told me he wanted to get there and home again so he hung on!"

The Jeter Crew passed Iwo Jima as they made their way to Chi Chi Jima that night, and they saw the firefight in progress, even though they were outside the 50-mile buffer zone they had to observe during the ground and sea battle. "It was lit up like the Fourth of July," recalled Weller. "(U.S.) Sea and ground forces were belting the central and northern part of Iwo; it was very evident even at 50 air miles away."

Weller's navigation got the plane to Chi Chi Jima, and radar man Dick David locked in on the target at about 2:50 a.m. Bombardier Greg Babykin had just released the load of 40-pound bombs when a burst of Japanese flak hit the No. 2 engine. The damage rendered the engine useless, so it had to be feathered (the prop turned so that it no longer catches the wind). It was really a problem because the No. 3 engine was already running rough and not pulling its weight. Consequently, the pilot was going to have to rely on engine Nos. 1 and 4 to get back through the black night to base. Jeter ordered all ammunition and flak suits jettisoned and asked Weller for an ETA (estimated time of arrival) for Guam. Saipan would have been closer but after checking the fuel, the crew knew they couldn't get to either Guam or Saipan with the reduced fuel efficiency resulting from the increased power needed from the two functioning engines.

It was one of those "oh my God!" moments you hope you won't ever have to face, but one that is almost inevitable in air combat, especially in the Pacific war where about 50 percent of the flyers didn't make it through. It's hard to imagine how these young guys felt at that moment. Fear and panic are emotions necessarily foreign to army pilots indoctrinated to believe they are invincible, indestructible and immune from the tragedy that strikes "the other guy." What the hell are they going to do?

Fortunately, the Jeter Crew drew on their training, experience and trusting relationships to keep themselves from falling into the drink aboard "the flying boxcar that didn't ditch well." The crew knew even if they survived a sea landing there were other dangers in the shark-infested and hopelessly vast Pacific Ocean held in Japanese hands. Chances were great that once in the water they would never be seen again like so many of their predecessors and successors. The dire circumstances demanded quick, clear thinking, and luckily such a commodity was abundant in that B-24J over Chi Chi Jima.

Ray Fritter, a waist gunner, was no doubt praying during these tense moments over Iwo Jima. Fritter, who became a Catholic priest after the war, inspired his fellow crew members and helped them through rough times. His prayers may have helped the crew make the right decision—democratically.

Although Frank Jeter was flight commander and could have unilaterally made the decision for the crew, he asked for the opinion of everyone on the flight deck, more evidence of the type of leader Jeter was. He was someone who allowed each player to be the master of his discipline. He was also, by all accounts, a skillful and confident pilot. To this day, the crew members praise Jeter for his leadership style, especially as exhibited that frightful night. Henderson recalled: "A conference was held on the flight deck, and we were unanimous that we did not want to ditch in the dark. Frank said, 'Let's take our chances with an emergency landing on Iwo. Radio Iwo and tell them we are coming in.' "

Everyone knew landing on Iwo Jima would be extremely risky, but they agreed it was their best chance to survive. "If we had ditched in the water, none of us would be here to tell about," said navigator John Weller. They also knew they were breaking the rules by getting within 50 air miles of Iwo Jima during the raging battle. Henderson tried relentlessly to make radio contact with the naval commander at Iwo Jima. He got no response. He established contact with San Francisco, Hawaii and Guam, but could not raise anyone at Iwo. In desperation, he sent an S.O.S message and the B-24's position "in the clear" on the standard airways frequency. That call meant that the Japanese could tune in to hear the Jeter Crew's attempts to contact the naval command ship at Iwo Jima.

As the Jeter Crew hung precariously in the night sky near the flaming battleground on Iwo Jima, tail gunner Doyle Ebel spotted an aircraft sneaking up on them from behind. Friend or foe, the crew didn't know. Another "Oh my God" moment ensued while the crew figured out from the partially lit markings that its stalker was a Black Widow, a P-61 U.S. fighter. But they weren't out of trouble yet. They still had to prove their friendly status to prevent the fighter from knocking them out of the air and into the sea.

Even though the B-24's IFF (identify friend or foe) equipment was sending the proper signals, the Black Widow pilot was not convinced. He ordered the Jeter Crew to send certain symbols from the "secret code of the day" by Aldis Lamp. Navigator John Weller explains: "Each day we were given a secret code that was placed in a canvas bag weighted down with lead. We were not to open the bag unless we needed to. If we went down, the code went to the bottom of the ocean so that the Japanese would not find it."

After Henderson flashed the code, the P-61 pilot flapped his wings, signifying to Jeter that he was convinced at last that the B-24 was a friendly craft. "Finally radio silence was broken, and we were given a compass heading to use for landing," recalled radio operator Dale Henderson. "We were told the runway was not lighted and was too short, but Frank radioed that we were committed and were going in." Weller adds: "They (the command ship) couldn't tell us the condition of the runway. It was a Japanese runway. They couldn't tell us that the Japs had mortared the runway that day, that it was full of mortar holes. They didn't tell us this because the Japanese had our frequency and they (the Japanese) knew what the hell was going on. They knew a plane was coming in."

Taking his chances on a beat-up landing strip that made no promises of suitability or kindness, pilot Frank Jeter let fate take command and began his impossible approach to Iwo Jima from the south. As he fishtailed the plane to slow it down over Mount Suribachi, what seemed like a miracle occurred. "There was an amazing American cease fire command," wrote Henderson. "All firing on the battleships, cruisers, destroyers and other ships and all the Marine heavy gun positions stopped on Iwo Jima. For the emergency landing, the Americans sent star shells to burst over the runway giving Frank and Herb the best available light."

"Frank and Herb did a masterful job of flying," recalled Weller. "I guess they saw Suribachi, which isn't very high. We knew the runway from having bombed Iwo (Jima) many times before the marine invasion. We knew that it started, not at the base of Suribachi, but awfully close. Frank stayed on the command ship radio frequency," recalled Weller. "We didn't know if they (naval commanders) were going to say anything to us (while the Japanese could eavesdrop). All we knew was that we were going down on this piece of ground. Frank told me: 'John, you stay on the intercom to communicate with the rest of the crew in the back end. You can let the guys know to get the hell out of the airplane if we have to bail out or if we crash or something.'

"We brought that thing down," recalled Weller. "And we were bouncing along the ground in and out of mortar holes. And then all of the sudden we saw a pile of crap, a pile of everything you can think of, at about 4,500 or 5,000 feet down the runway. Normally to land a B-24 you want 6,000 to 8,000 feet minimum," Weller said. Adding to the treachery of the night landing, the Japanese harassed the crippled aircraft with mortars and small arms fire as the 11 boys of the Jeter Crew bounded violently down the too-short runway in what some have called a "Flying Coffin."

"These two men (pilot Jeter and co-pilot Herb Harter) had their harnesses on, and they literally stood up on the brakes of that 24 and stopped that thing right in front of the pile of crap. We didn't crash into it," recalled Weller.

Years later, Weller met a marine sergeant whose gun station

was near the runway and saw the Jeter Crew come in just 20 feet above his head. John Farritor, 1st Sgt., Charlie Battery, 1st Battalion, 12th Marine Regiment, was positioned along the west side of the airstrip, 100 yards from the south end. He recalled the surprising cease fire command and marveled at the silence. Farritor recalled in a letter years later: "That cease fire silenced 48 artillery pieces on Iwo Jima, plus over 300 Navy ships at sea around Iwo Jima. Fleet Admiral (Chester W.) Nimitz and (Marine) General Holland McTyeire 'Howlin' Mad' Smith made the decision to order the cease fire in minutes, not hours. Looking back it was the only command that would save the crew and the plane, and the Navy had every reason for being 'trigger happy' after all Kamikaze planes had sunk a carrier and damaged other ships just off Iwo Jima.

"The quietness of Iwo Jima was unreal, after 20 plus days of the din of battle. Because of the size of the island, all the artillery was concentrated in a very small area. Then the flares started bursting in air alongside the airstrip, and my No. 1 man yelled 'Look!' That was when the plane showed up over Suribachi. We really thought it was going to land on us." Farritor remembers his ammunition man mumbling a prayer as the Jeter Crew came in. "I asked him if he was praying for the crew, and he said: 'No, I'm praying it will miss us!' "

"As soon as we landed the firing began again," Dale Henderson wrote. "It seemed to come from everywhere. The ships were firing into Jap positions in the middle and northern parts of the island. The Marine batteries were firing over the runway into positions that were all too close. We were flyboys in the midst of a ground battle. We knew from nothing. We were out of our element, and we didn't even know where the front lines were."

It might have felt good to be on solid earth after their harrowing landing on Iwo Jima, but the Jeter Crew was still anything but safe. They were acutely aware they could still be killed by a flying shell coming from either the Japanese or the Americans. One round hitting the Jeter craft's 1,000-gallon fuel supply and the boys could be incinerated. They looked around and saw a

47

Catalina aircraft parked off to the side of the runway, the only familiar looking object in the darkness. They pulled up and stopped next to it.

Frank and Herb jumped out of the cockpit and headed off to find someone who could tell them what to do next. Frank left Weller in charge of the rest of the crew, knowing full well that he and Herb's chances of coming back were not good. They walked over to a lean-to near the runway and poked their heads in. Inside the marine in charge greeted them with: "Don't you know there's a war going on here?" He told them to get back into their plane and lay low until dawn. When Frank told the marine that the Jeter craft was carrying about 1,000 gallons of fuel, the marine said: "If you get hit, you'll never know it."

Having landed at 3:50 a.m., the boys had about three hours to hold tight until daybreak. The crew's plan was to sleep but Weller doesn't recall actually dosing off. "You couldn't really find a space to lay out in a B-24. Years later when my family saw a B-24 they couldn't believe that we flew in those things. They wondered how we ever got into them because the interior spaces were so tight."

The boys felt a little better when dawn came, knowing they would be able to investigate the lay of the land. Each of them instinctively realized that during their dark, death-defying ordeal they had forged an even stronger bond and had indeed become brothers for life.

The first sight they saw was the surface of the volcanic, battle-torn, smoldering island. Dale laughed when he saw a pipe stuck into the gaseous sand with the message: "Take your first hot shower here." Today their job was to get their bearings, re-group and figure a way to get back to Guam, hopefully in their fully functioning B-24.

Henderson, with his philosophical bent, pondered the denuded and smelly state of the island he saw close up for the first time. "It was a kind of weird feeling to look skyward and realize that just a few short weeks earlier we had been flying over and bombing the very spot where we were now standing." Doyle and Dick, said to be the best scroungers in the Air Corps, gathered up some K-rations while Sam Tillery and Ray Fritter built a fire to combat the chill of the overcast morning. They had instant coffee, canned eggs and ham, crackers and part of a chocolate bar while they collected their wits to face the next challenge: repairing their B-24.

In their morning visit to the Marine command center, Frank and Herb learned that C-46 air ambulances were taking the wounded from Iwo Jima to Guam, Saipan and Tinian hospitals during daylight hours. That meant they could have the engine they needed brought to them by a C-46 on its return flight to Iwo Jima the next morning to pick up more casualties. "We began to gather tools, some from the Marines but most of what we needed from a P-51 squadron that was just beginning to fly in. We acquired a hoist (and A-frame) from them and went to work," Henderson wrote.

Jeter put Bob Larson and nose gunner Vic Crowell in charge of the repair of the aircraft. After all, Larson, the engineer, had worked at Consolidated Aircraft in Long Beach, California, before the war and knew the B-24 inside out. Larson ran into a challenge when he tried to get a particular prop wrench from the P-51 crew. "I told the guys 'you gotta get it. I don't care how you get it but we have to have it,'" Larson said with a voice that conveyed a sense of urgency even 60 years after the fact. "Well, they got it," Larson told film producer Grace Provenzano. By evening, Larson and crew had removed the prop and were ready for the engine.

On the morning of the 14th, the ambulance brought the B-24 engine, two mechanics and a prop man. Henderson recalls: the prop man wasn't happy that Larson had removed the prop, but he had to admit Larson had done a good job." The Jeter Crew worked the rest of the 14th and 15th getting the new engine installed and in good working order. "It wasn't often that a flying crew was required to do such work. Everyone pitched in; we all did the jobs Larson assigned." Years later, Larson recalled: "It was just do-it-yourself in the dirt."

On the 16th, the crew fired up the new engine at 7:15 and let it idle. "At 7:30, we took off from that short runway. Again, Frank and Herb did a great piece of flying. We cleared the end of the runway and roared over the Jap lines. We took a couple of (small arms) rounds but there was no damage. We landed on Guam at

12:30 p.m. March 16, completing a combat mission of 87 hours, one of the longest (in time) in the war."

Here is Henderson's understated log account for the death-defying mission over Iwo Jima:

"Night snooper. Takeoff at 21:30, just as bombs away at 02:50 flak hit #2, #3 running rough. Against orders, skipper decided to make emergency landing at Iwo. Could not raise field by radio, night fighter looked us over. Landed 03:50, (Japanese) mortared field as we landed. Stayed on Iwo until 07:30 3/16/45, 3 ½ days. Experience none will forget. I looked for Harold (Frackelton, boyhood chum); he was killed two days before. His buddies, great guys, as were all marines. Flew in engine which we had to change. Larson did great job. Landed 12:20. Combat time: 11:10 (for this mission). Total combat time: 193.03 (for all their missions so far)."

Within three days, the Jeter Crew was back in the air flying another mission to Chi Chi Jima. Their misadventure was not even a blip in the furious course of war under way in the Pacific Theater. With all Iwo Jima radio communications suspended overnight, there was no official record of their landing on Iwo Jima until much later. Doyle Ebel notes, however, that the dramatic departure from routine was recorded on his Individual Flight Record simply as a landing on Iwo Jima during a mission to Chi Chi Jima on March 12, 1945, and a takeoff for Guam on March 16, 1945.

Weller said he learned later from Navy records that the Naval Command Ship El Dorado detected the passing of an aircraft over Iwo Jima that night, but they couldn't say for sure it was the Jeter Crew. "They said it might have been us, or it might have been somebody else," Weller recounted. "But I don't know who else would have been up there at the time," he said with a hearty laugh.

Decades later, after rediscovering forgotten footage of their wartime experiences, members of the crew became interested in documenting their adventures and sharing them with the world. Gathered at an 11th Bombardment Group reunion in 1979, they encountered two marines in Central City, Colorado, also attending a reunion, who remembered Frank and Herb coming to their lean-to and asking for directions. "I could just kick myself in the fanny," Weller says. "I didn't think to ask their names."

Weller picked up his search for documentation later by contacting Marine groups known to have been on the island. He eventually found Farritor and others who wrote letters about their memories of the night the troubled B-24 hobbled onto Iwo Jima during a momentary cease fire. These letters, as well as a certificate from the D-Day Museum in New Orleans signed by author/historian Stephen Ambrose, serve as the official record of the Jeter Crew's emergency landing on Iwo Jima.

Doyle Ebel gives a B-24 some TLC on Guam.

Tent housing on Guam. *Photos courtesy of the Jeter Crew.*

Above, Dale Henderson, left, and John Weller at target practice. At right, Doyle Ebel doing his washing on Guam. *Photos courtesy of the Jeter Crew.*

A Consolidated B-24 from the 42nd Bomb Squad takes off from Guam while an airman climbs a palm tree to hang a communications line, January 1945. *U.S. Air Force photo.*

Top photo, Whitey Whiteside, a navigator who surprised himself by delivering a healthy native Chamorro baby boy in a hurry on Guam. Whiteside was summoned to the birth scene by the baby's father, who stopped him on the road as Whitey made his way back to camp from a drinking party.

At left, Jeter Crew navigator John Weller on Guam, 1945. Weller got to know Whiteside in navigation school. *Photos courtesy of the Jeter Crew.*

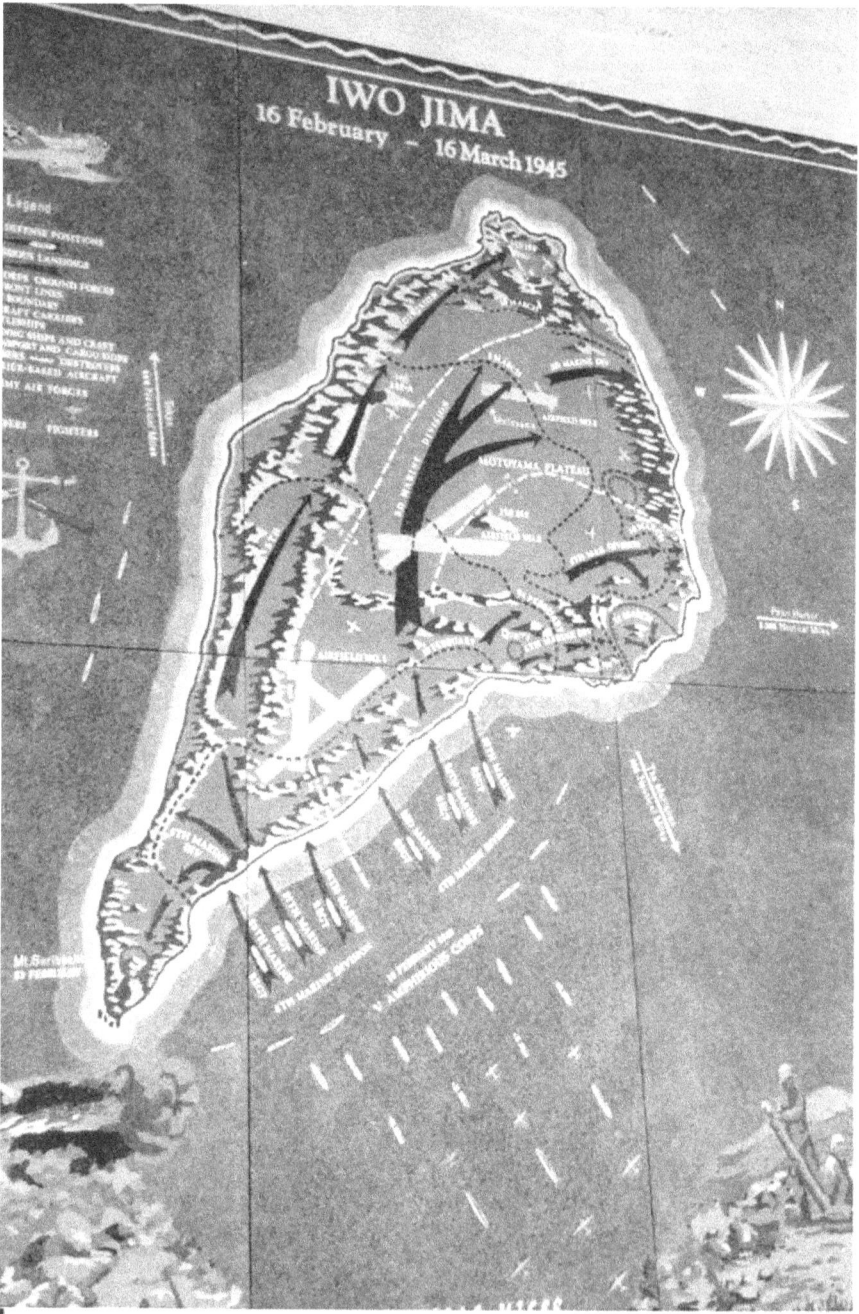

An exhibit at the National World War II Museum in New Orleans shows the game plan for invasion of Iwo Jima, February 1945. *Photo by Virginia McPartland.*

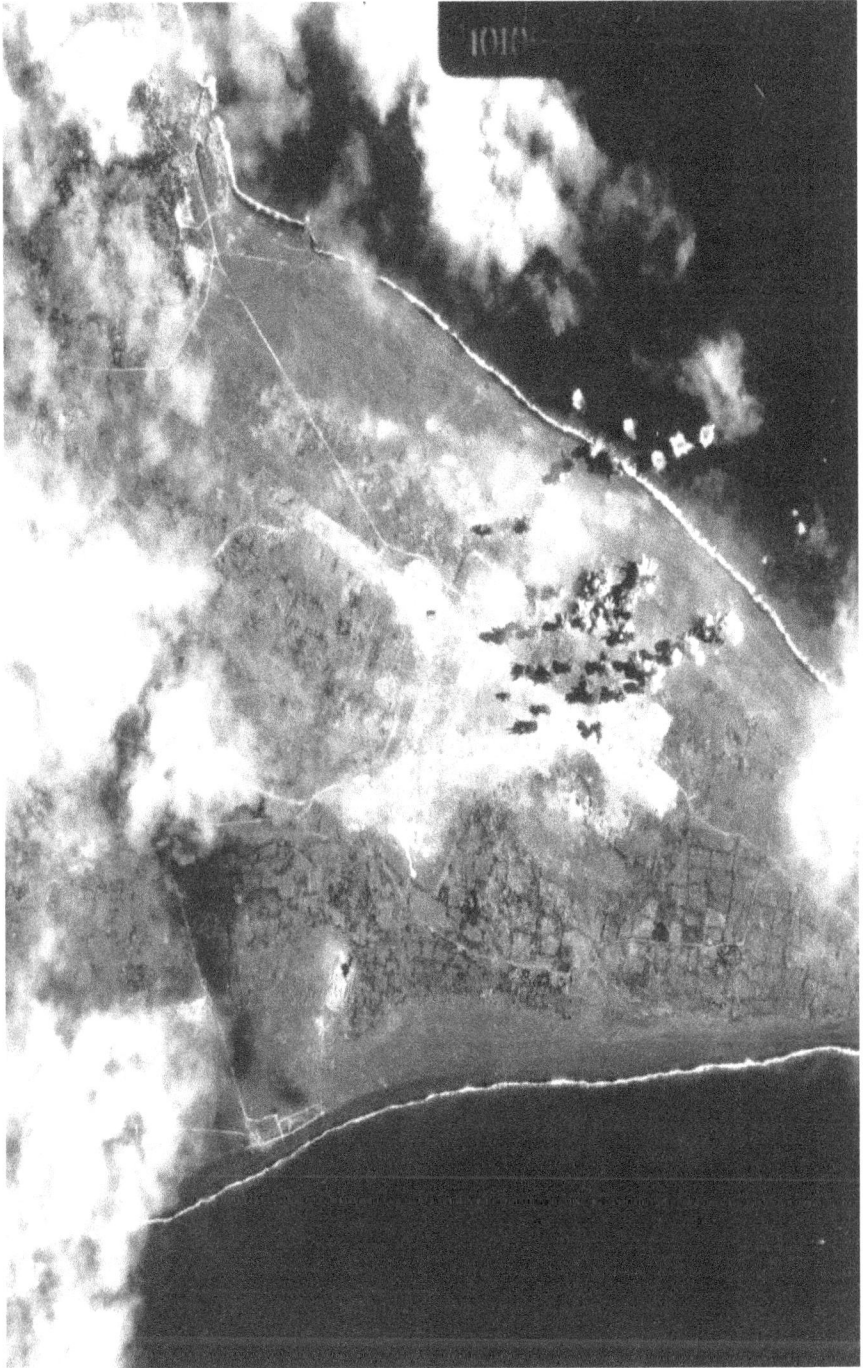

The Jeter Crew's view of Iwo Jima after bombs away on their mission on December 12, 1944. *Photo from the Dale Henderson collection.*

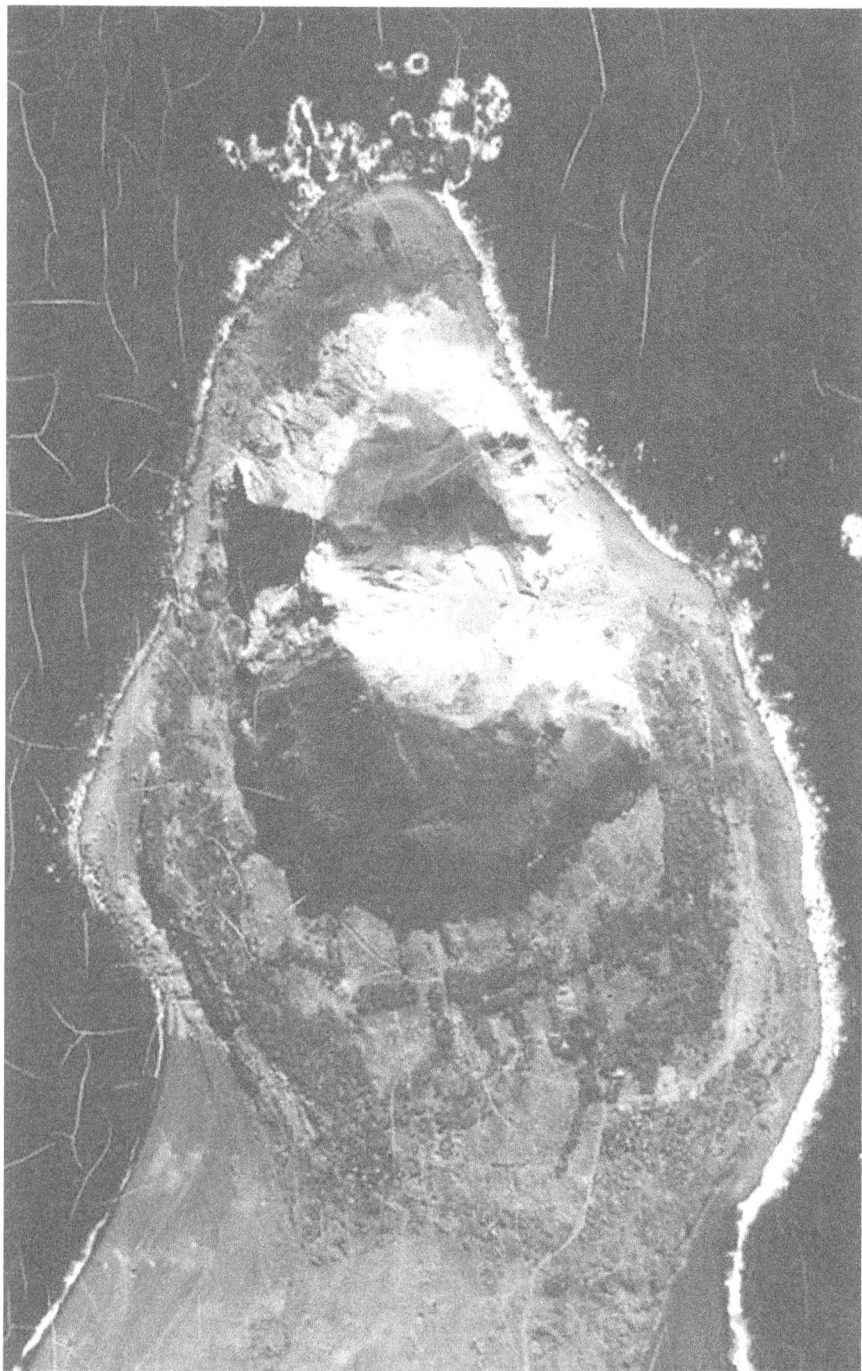

View of Mt. Suribachi on Iwo Jima during the Jeter Crew mission on January 27, 1945. *Photo from the Dale Henderson collection.*

Bombing of Chi Chi Jima, December 27, 1944. The Jeter Crew had just hit this target when they lost an engine and had to land on Iwo Jima in the middle of a firefight on March 13, 1945. *Photo from the Dale Henderson collection.*

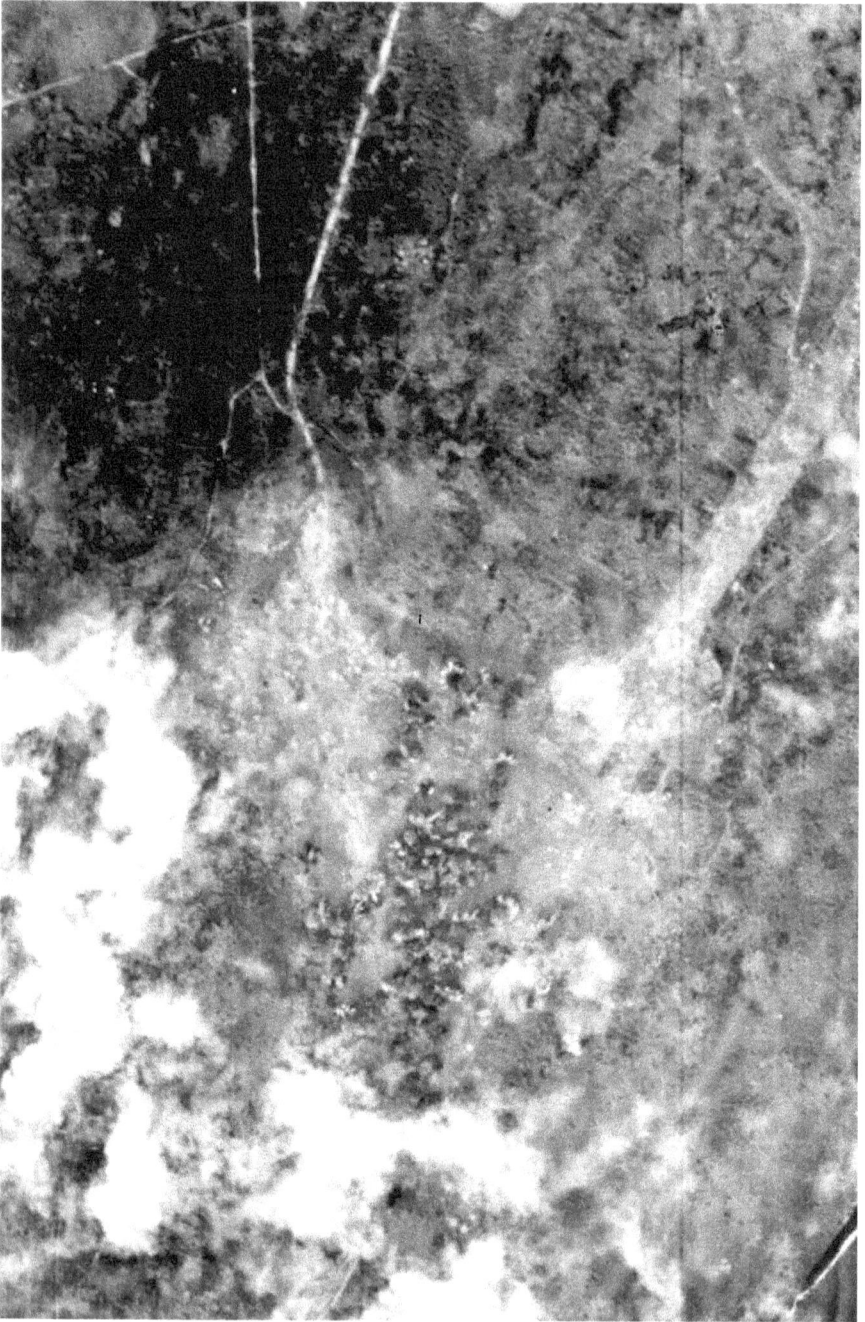

Bombing of Iwo Jima airstrip January 30, 1945. *Photo from the Dale Henderson collection.*

A 26th Bomb Squad B-24 leaves behind a flaming Iwo Jima beachhead. Mt. Suribachi can be seen over the bomber's left wing.

Precise pounding of Iwo Jima airstrip by B-24 bombers of the Seventh Air Force, February, 1945. The Jeter Crew landed their crippled B-24 on the plundered runway a month later. *U.S. Air Force photos.*

61

The pilot of a P-61 Black Widow fighter plane (like the one shown above) stalked the Jeter Crew's B-24 as a possible enemy craft when the Jeter boys were desperately looking for a place to land on Iwo Jima.

Seventh Air Force bombing of Iwo Jima. Airfield Jeter Crew landed on barely visible under black smoke and white clouds in right upper center. *U.S. Air Force photo.*

The morning after their emergency landing, the Jeter boys enjoyed a campfire and some breakfast on smoldering, battle-torn Iwo Jima. Pictured here from left, Ray Fritter, Dick David, Doyle Ebel, Herb Harter, Dale Henderson; in front, Greg Babykin and John Weller.

From left: Dick David, Doyle Ebel and Sam Tillery on Iwo Jima, March 13, 1945. *Photos courtesy of the Jeter Crew.*

Top photo, Vic Crowell perches on top of the damaged engine as other crew members approach the repair from the sides and bottom. Above left, U.S. Air Force photo shows the air tower on Iwo Jima. Above right, Sam Tillery with arm outreached. *Top and right photos courtesy of the Jeter Crew.*

Bodies of Japanese soldiers littered the Iwo Jima landscape after the last Banzai charge, March 1945.

The carcass of a Japanese fighter plane crashed on Iwo Jima, March 1945. *U.S. Air Force photos.*

CHAPTER 6: BATTLE OF IWO — HORROR ON THE GROUND

The Battle of Iwo Jima had been raging for almost a month by the time the Jeter Crew landed its crippled B-24 bomber on the smoldering island in the wee hours of March 13, 1945. By then, 4,000 Americans and at least as many Japanese soldiers had been killed in what would be one of the fiercest and bloodiest battles in the Pacific Theater.

The U.S. Marines and Navy had launched a huge invasion of the 8-square mile island from 450 ships on February 19, more than three weeks before. With the help of U. S. Navy aerial bombers and offshore artillery, the marines had secured Mount Suribachi and most of the rest of the island. But the battle was not yet won, and many more soldiers on both sides would die before it was finally over on March 26.

In the end, the Japanese, whose soldiers' creed called for a fight to the death, lost 21,000 men out of a total of 22,000 that first greeted the American fighting force. The U.S lost 6,800 men, the largest loss in any battle in American history; U.S. Iwo Jima casualties (injuries and deaths) totaled about 27,000.

The Japanese had prepared well for the U.S. amphibious invasion. They had installed 750 defense installations — pillboxes, anti-aircraft artillery, anti-tank guns — all hidden in rocks, caves and within Mount Suribachi. The honey-combed mountain had 1,000 cave entrances and pillboxes (gun stations dug within the rock or enclosed in cement).

When the marines landed, they soon realized that the Japanese defenders had mostly been spared from the pre-invasion attacks by staying underground in 13,000 yards of tunnels and caves. Every rock, every grain of black volcanic sand, and most every plant on the island had been upended by U.S. bombs. But most soldiers were alive and ready to fight the invading Americans. (The roughly 1,000 Japanese civilians who once called the destroyed village of Motoyama home had been evacuated before the bombing began.)

For the Jeter Crew — and many other crews who had risked their lives bombing Iwo Jima — the realization that their missions were largely ineffective was disheartening. "We were very disappointed that we hadn't done the damage we wanted to. Nobody knew the Japanese were buried under the ground," navigator John Weller recalled.

With the legendary raising of the American flag on Mount Suribachi on February 23, most people around the world believed the island, considered crucial to the continuing Pacific campaign, was in American hands. Strangely about a month later, two commanders would prematurely call the epic battle over — Navy Admiral Chester Nimitz on March 14 — and Marine General Harry Schmidt on the 16th — ironically while the Jeter Crew was on the island repairing its aircraft (March 13 to March 16).

On the morning of the Jeter Crew's emergency landing on Iwo Jima, radio man Dale Henderson greeted the dawn with optimism: "Even though the morning was overcast, the day seemed brighter."

But in the light of day Henderson could see the effects of warfare: "We had a view of a volcanic island that had been stripped of vegetation and structures," Henderson wrote in his memoir. He looked skyward and recalled the Jeter Crew's bombing raids over the island in the previous months. Their missions had been part of a massive 7th Air Force bombing plan to drop 5,800 tons of explosives in 2,700 sorties during a 70-day period prior to the invasion. Weller remembered: "We were blasting the hell out of that piece of land (a few weeks earlier)." The Navy had also bombarded the island with all its sea and air power in the last three days before the ground troops attacked.

What the Jeter flyboys saw when the sun came up over Iwo Jima that day was like nothing most of them had ever seen before. Except for radar man Dick David, none of the crew had seen war up close. From the air, they couldn't see the damage they wreaked with their bombs. From their B-24, the targets may not have seemed real. These boys never had actually come face to face with blood and guts, burning flesh and dismembered bodies.

Not only was the island denuded of most vegetation, it smelled of the yellow sulfur mist that exuded from its cracks. Smoke from the Marine flame throwers' charred targets and exploded mortars, shells and grenades created a smoggy, muggy and hot atmosphere on the island. Add to that the smell of burning and rotting dead bodies and the resemblance to a vision of hell is undeniable.

Feeling a bit cocky after the success of the emergency landing, and a little bored, John Weller came up with an idea. Why not take advantage of the situation to see what the ground war looked like?

Remember, this is a young man who left his sophomore year at college in San Jose, California, to go to war. The Pacific islands he'd seen from the ground—Oahu, Johnston, Kwajalein, Palmyra, Guam, and Maui—were mostly devoid of violence and some could even be called peaceful.

The Jeter Crew members had seen danger many times: they had been shot at routinely on their bombing missions, seen other crews go down, and they had dodged bombs dropped on Saipan during their stay there. But none of this could have prepared John Weller for what he saw next.

"Now I'll be the first one to admit this was a stupid thing for me to do. Absolutely stupid. You know I was 21 or 22 at the time; we all felt pretty invincible. Nothing was going to get us. Nothing! You get that attitude. You have to have that attitude.

"I had nothing to do before we brought the engine in. So I saw a marine there, a captain, and I said: 'What the heck is this war all about?' He said 'Get your helmet, get your .45 and I'll take you up there.' I says 'okay, we'll see what it's all about.' "

Weller climbed into a jeep with the marine captain, and they drove up to an area at the center of Iwo Jima where organized Japanese resistance had been vanquished and the marines were "mopping up". There, the tender young man briefly took in the horrific war scene: "I could hear guns going off. I saw dead people lying on the ground. (The marine) said: 'watch out for land mines . . . don't step there.'

"I could hear just a horrible sound. They were using flame throwers (to clear out pockets of resistance), and flame throwers make kind of a whooshing sound . . . I wasn't up there more than 30 seconds or maybe a minute maximum, and I said to him, 'get me out of here. Take me back.' "

Weller's unplanned excursion to the battle zone might qualify as his worst memory of the war. On the day of his tour, the marines had a number of operations under way on various portions of the small island. The 24th marines received orders to continue mopping up operations, burying enemy dead, collecting their own dead and policing assigned areas.

In Area 182, just north of Airfield No. 1 and likely the zone Weller visited, the 24th marines were patrolling but found no enemy activity. Meanwhile the 25th marines (battalion) were encountering "very strong resistance that consisted chiefly of mortar fire and intense machine gun fire from well camouflaged pillboxes," according to the Third Marine Division's official battle reports of the day.

"When the flame thrower tank made its final run of the day and fired up one of the draws inland from the beach road, it caught a large number of the enemy in the open. Of this group of enemy at least 75 were killed by the flames and machine gun fire from the tank, and by (the battalion's) fire when the (Japanese) ran out of the draw."

At this stage of the battle, flame throwers were the weapon of choice: "The 2nd battalion had use of a large flame thrower tank which belonged to the Fifth Marine Division and used it to excellent advantage. This tank," the marines report said, "which shoots a flame about 125 yards, proved to be the weapon that worked when all others failed. Its long flame range and the area covered by one burst contributed to its remarkable success."

The daily report continues: "Enemy resistance continued to be fanatical to the end. The enemy remains in his positions to the last. Flame throwing tanks are the only weapon that has ever caused the enemy to break and run. Some enemy have been observed running out in front of our lines and committing suicide by holding grenades to their heads.

"Several instances have been observed of the enemy (hidden) in spider-trap fox holes having large satchel charges (explosives in a bag), which they threw at whatever might pass their holes. If they were observed before this could be accomplished, they blew themselves up. Hand-placed charges are being used against our tanks, causing (operators) to work in pairs. Tanks flushed about 75 of the enemy from a cave, and a number of these (soldiers) were reported to have jumped off a high cliff in that sector."

When the resurrected Jeter Crew craft took off from Iwo Jima at 7:30 a.m. March 16, the marines were continuing their quest to eliminate all remaining enemy pockets on the island. As a last gasp on March 26, the Japanese mustered one final attack, targeting U.S. Army fighter pilots and ground crews who were bivouacked southwest of Iwo Jima's Airfield No. 2.

"The Japanese came out of their hiding places in the northern end of the island. That they knew this was to be their last fight was evident by their dress. Some officers, of whom there were many, wore clean white shirts; their swords were highly polished. One was a doctor; others were enlisted medicos. Some carried American rifles and grenades taken from dead marines."

When the Japanese reached the fighter encampment: "All hell broke loose. Fighter pilots awakened to the crackle of gunfire and exploding grenades. The Japanese charged into tents, slashing their way forward with their swords and hurling grenades.

"Barefooted and helmetless, the (Fifth Marine Battalion) Pioneers scrambled out of their holes to attack with rifles and grenades of their own. One marine, unable to find his rifle in the semi-darkness, charged off to the attack armed with a screwdriver.

"When the battle was over the Pioneers counted 196 enemy dead and collected forty swords. Enemy survivors who sought to escape back to their caves were mercilessly hunted down and exterminated with grenades. The cost to the Pioneers was nine dead and forty wounded," the marines' daily report concluded.

Ironically, on the same day of this attack, the U.S. officially claimed the victory of the Battle of Iwo Jima. By this date, U.S. B-29 bombers were already using Iwo Jima's airfields to take off for fire bombing missions to mainland Japan.

After the harrowing experience over and on Iwo Jima March 12-16, 1945, the Jeter Crew found themselves quickly back into action. On March 19, they flew a day mission over Chi Chi Jima, the treacherous object of the March 12 night mission. This time they returned safely to Guam without a glitch.

On March 24, they mounted their first attack on Marcus, an even more dreaded target. Henderson's log reads: "First mission against this rock. No, thank you! It's rough. Gunners just fire for elevation. The island is so small only three planes could go in at a time." During the attack, Japanese gunners were ferocious and aimed 25 bursts against the Jeter Crew. Five hit their mark tearing holes in the plane. One shot came two inches from radio man Dale Henderson's head and went out the top. "(There was a) U.S. sub on the surface about 20 miles off the rock to pick up crews of damaged planes," Henderson wrote. "(Greg) Babykin really laid them in there. Two 1,000 lbs hit the target area that was only 20-feet by 60-feet."

The Marcus mission a success, the crew landed uneventfully back at Guam about 6:30 that evening after 11 hours of combat time. After debriefing, they were told they were going on rest, well deserved and overdue after 200 hours of high-tension combat. A few minutes later, they grabbed their bags and boarded a C-47 cargo plane bound for Hickam Field, Oahu.

CHAPTER 7: GOOD TIMES: REST AND RECREATION ON OAHU

In a few short hours on December 7, 1941, Hawaii's Pearl Harbor became a historic, monumental place, a place where America was violated and drawn into a world war nobody wanted. For the Jeter Crew, it was and still is a place of great contrasts. A place of great horror and a place of great pleasure. They passed over its waters on their way out to battle in the expansive Pacific Theater in November 1944. In late March of 1945, after four months of taking their chances against the fanatically fighting Japanese, they passed over again on their way to Hickam Field and the then-peaceful and nurturing environs of the island of Oahu. The crew had trained at Kahuku Army Air Base on the northern Oahu shore, so the island was familiar. Near Hickam Field, the Red Cross ran a rest camp for fatigued airmen like the Jeter Crew.

For what happily turned out to be an entire month (March 26 to April 29, 1945), the Jeter boys could take refuge from the slings and arrows of intense war. They could leave behind the scrambling for fox-hole cover when Japanese bombs dropped near them on Saipan. They could leave behind the anti-aircraft fire that punctuated their perilous missions over targets such as Iwo Jima, Chi Chi Jima, Truk and Marcus. They could act like normal boys, normal American boys *on vacation.*

The Jeter Crew's R&R in Hawaii didn't come any too soon. At the time, they didn't realize or understand that after 23 bombing missions, they might be on the verge of battle fatigue. If their experience was true to military statistics, they could easily have cracked up if they hadn't gotten a reprieve. "Everyone has a breaking point," Doyle Ebel acknowledged almost 70 years later.

For the 20-hour flight to Hawaii, the boys climbed into the back of the aircraft that had no seats, only aluminum benches along the sides, and tried to sleep.

The plane landed on Kwajalein for refueling at dawn the next day. "We were told we had one hour to eat and do whatever else we had to do," tail gunner Doyle Ebel said. Later in the day, they stopped on Johnston Island where the refueling was quick; and the plane arrived at Oahu about 9 that night. By the time they arrived at Hickam Field, the crew was hungry, sleepy and scruffy, as well as emotionally and physically exhausted.

The first order of business was food, and a Red Cross canteen was open and obliging with coffee and donuts. "We were a raunchy looking bunch," recalled Doyle. "Our clothes were wrinkled, our hair was a mess. We hadn't had a shave, our clothes were half worn out, and I'm sure we smelled raunchy. There was a young lady there who was about 19 or 20 years old. Well, we hadn't seen a lady for over a year, and she had on some of the best smelling perfume. So I said to the other guys, 'come on over and smell this,' so we were sniffing around her like a bunch of hound dogs! Everyone else there was spic and polished. They must have thought we were terrible."

Pilot Frank Jeter arranged for a truck to take the crew to the rest camp adjacent to Hickam Field. The Red Cross-operated facility had a large open-air pavilion that featured a stage for entertainment, a dance floor, and a socializing area with bamboo tables and chairs. They also had a beer garden that was open from 5 to 10 p.m. and a room with billiard and ping pong tables. Often there were dances and shows on the weekends. The crew was free to go into Honolulu to partake of the city's offerings of entertainment, food and culture, including the already famous, yet primitive Waikiki Beach. But they were not allowed to go in until they got new regulation clothes. Doyle remembered: "Our clothes were so ragged we couldn't go into the city until we were issued new uniforms. We had to take them to the cleaners and have them pressed, and we had to have all our chevrons and patches sewn on. In the combat zone, nobody wore their chevrons, it didn't matter what your rank was. But once we got to Oahu, we had to be in full uniform."

Expecting to spend only 10 days on rest, the Jeter boys were excited to learn they would get a real break from duty — 35 days on Oahu. The B-29s' firebombing of Japanese cities was in full force, and B-24 bombing crews were low on the priority list for fuel and ammunition and for air transportation back to Guam. "We didn't care. We were having a big time over there. It was all right with us to stay longer," Doyle continued. "The only problem was we were livin' it up and spent all our money. We got paid once while we were there but we ran out again. So Frank arranged for us to get an advance in pay to last through the leave."

Getting around the island could be challenging because the boys didn't have access to a vehicle. They usually had to hitch-hike or rely on the daily mail truck to take them to Honolulu in the morning and bring them back to the base in the evening. Obviously, that curbed their ability to roam the island and explore its many hidden treasures and pleasures. One such gem was a pristine, largely undiscovered and unmapped 45-foot-high water-fall and remote pool in Waimea Valley on the northwest side of the island. "It wasn't called 'Waimea Falls' at that time," Doyle recalled. "We didn't know what to call it. We just called it our 'swimming hole.' There was nothing there. We had to cut through the jungle to get there," Doyle recalled.[4]

The Jeter boys had visited the waterfall a few times while they were stationed at Kahuku Air Base for training in 1944, and they wanted to get back there and luxuriate in its beauty again while on rest.

"We knew how to get there: You took the road along the beach to the bridge over the creek that leads to the falls. We knew the way. We would just follow the water to the falls." But not having a vehicle was an obstacle they had to overcome.

Social events gave the boys the opportunity to meet girls, women who were part of the Women's Army Corps (WAC) and Army nurses. One flirtation took hold after Dale Henderson met his future wife, Bernice Messer, a WAC on Oahu. Bernice brought

---

4 In contrast, the Waimea Valley today is a developed park with botanical gardens of native plants, revered ancestral sites, and highly organized activities, including hikes and weddings. In 2004, a developer had plans to build a private estate there and close off the 18-acre valley to the public. The native Hawaiians fought the plan and the Audubon Society, state of Hawaii and others bought the property and it's now run by a nonprofit corporation with a charter to keep the land natural and open to the public.

her friends along for parties and the boys often had the company of the opposite sex, an obvious thrill after being isolated in a combat zone. Sam Tillery, the ball turret gunner, attracted women on his own, according to crew members who say he was a ladies' man.

Bernice and her WAC friends were also able to help when it came to getting transportation and special food. She had a friend who worked for the motor pool who was able to get them a truck for trips to the swimming hole (and elsewhere). But who was going to drive? No one had a GI driver's license. Luckily, Dick David, who had been in the Army infantry at Guadalcanal, had a bit more savvy than the others about how to cut through the military red tape. Bernice got the form for Dick who filled it out in his "perfect" handwriting using the appropriate language and code numbers and forging the signature of one of his superiors from an earlier assignment. He dated it 1944. The problem was that it looked too fresh and clean to be believable. "We had to make it look kinda old. So we put it on the floor and rubbed it around, roughed it up, and then Dick took it outside and put it in a flower bed and got it a little dirty," Doyle recalled. The fake license fooled the motor pool staff, and the crew was soon on its way to Waimea Valley and the swimming hole, carrying a huge picnic lunch the girls acquired from the WAC mess hall!

Using pilot Frank Jeter's movie camera, crew members took turns filming their lives at war—and at rest. A short film of one of the group's rowdy parties at Waimea Falls survived the war and lives as a testament to the crew's great time of relaxation on Oahu. The quality of the film is good enough to see that all in attendance were enjoying the effects of alcohol and the lack of any stress while the war raged elsewhere.

Posing for the camera, the crew members stood still long enough for a precious moment of togetherness and joy to be immortalized. Vic Crowell, nose gunner and youngest of the crew, was hopping around like a jelly bean wearing swim trunks, a Hawaiian print shirt, and a hat borrowed from one of the officers. Bernice and Dale can be seen clearly as a couple on the verge of falling in love. Ironically, three months later, Dale would be involved in a horrific plane crash on Okinawa that would scar him for life and delay his release from the service until August of 1946. The couple married in November of 1945 while he was still recovering from his injuries.

While on leave on Oahu, co-pilot Herb Harter and navigator John Weller were invited to spend a week on Coconut Isle, a private estate off the east shore of Oahu that had been turned into an officers' retreat during the war. The pre-war owner, Christian Holmes II, an heir to the Fleischmann Yeast fortune, had more than doubled the small 12-acre island with crushed rubble, sand and dirt during the 1930s. Holmes had built a residence, aquaria, kennels and aviaries for his many pets.

When John and Herb were there, the 28-acre island was set up with luxurious accommodations and a Red Cross staff that attended to their every need. The food and drink was the best, John Weller says, in great contrast to the mess hall on Guam and the cold sandwiches on their target-bound B-24 Liberator.

Coconut Island, now owned by the state, is the Hawaii Institute of Marine Biology, part of the University of Hawaii. The institute has the distinction of being the only American laboratory built on a coral reef. The island provided the backdrop for "Gilligan's Island," a popular American TV comedy produced in the 1960s.

John and Herb were also invited to spend a week on Maui at the home of Gordon Lightner, MD, a physician who took care of employees of the Alexander & Baldwin Company, which owned some of the largest plantations on the Hawaiian Islands. "The Lightners were wonderful hosts," John writes years later. "They had a housekeeper who gently rapped on our door to ask us what we wanted for breakfast and when we would be down to enjoy.

"Every night was party night. We enjoyed good food and spirits as well as meeting fun people like Judge Edna Jenkins, the local judge for Waimea, and her friend, a local colonel.

"The Lightners gave us a full-fledged luau complete with live band and roasted pig. They invited their friends to meet us and took care of our dates for the evening. They instructed Herb and me to greet people as they arrived and act as hosts. My date arrived with her parents, the Baldwins. Jane was a beautiful girl, golden hair, suntanned in a white, long dress. We had an enjoyable evening talking and dancing. There was a 10 o'clock curfew on Maui, so everyone left (at that time).

"Dr. Lightner, who resembled actor Sydney Greenstreet in appearance, settled back in his big chair and asked me if I had a good time. I said that it was great and my date was a real knockout. He laughed and asked me how old I thought Jane was. I said 18 or 19 years. He said Jane was 14, and (I thought) if he had told me earlier, I would not have had a great evening; after all, I was 22. I think Herb's date was as nice and probably as young, although he says he doesn't remember!

"It was an interesting time for all of us. Dr. Lightner, earlier in time, had operated on one of the Tokyo Rose broadcasters when she lived on Maui. He wasn't too pleased he had contributed to her well-being!" John wrote.

As luck would have it, Dick David's 22nd birthday just happened to be on April 23, 1945, one of the last days the Jeter Crew was on rest on Oahu. A good reason to party, everyone agreed. But this would be special—a surprise party complete with wine, good food and a birthday cake scrounged by Doyle and Dale from the WAC's mess. To orchestrate the surprise, Doyle was picked to take Dick into Honolulu for the day while the others got everything ready for the evening party. Frank got burgundy wine and Bernice's WAC friends helped with more liquor and food. Sam Tillery contributed by bringing a few extra girls.

During the month-long leave, the Jeter Crew didn't just party. Several airmen pursued their own interests while in a wonderful bubble that kept them pretty much war-proof. Ray Fritter, the waist gunner who later became a Catholic priest, got on a surf board and challenged himself to learn to ride the Hawaiian surf. Doyle and Dale sometimes stood on Waikiki Beach and watched as Ray tried to get up on the board. They also hung around various small cafes and bars on the beach that was almost empty of hotels or tourist activities. The only two hotels at the time were the Royal Hawaiian and the Moana Hotel. Bob Larson, a farmer at heart, took a job in the sugar cane fields, one way to forget the stress of replacing a shot-up B-24 engine in a war zone (as he had done on Iwo Jima.)

While on rest, the crew also contemplated the completion of the requisite 40 bombing missions. They realized that they needed to score some liquor for the party they would host when their war experience drew to a close. "Dale and I were always conniving," Doyle admitted. "If there was an opportunity (to get liquor), we would take advantage of it." Always thinking, Doyle came up with a scheme to trade their furlough gasoline allotments for liquor. He explained: "We knew a woman who worked for the OPA (Office of Price Administration, the agency that handled wartime rationing), and I asked her if it was true that you could get five gallons of gasoline with furlough papers. She said 'yes,' so I asked her if she would trade me five gallons of gasoline for a bottle of liquor. She said 'sure.' But when I presented her with about 10 furlough papers, she said 'whoa, I can't do that. Why don't you just come to my house? My boyfriend always brings me a bottle and I've got a lot.' Well, as it turned out, we got 13 bottles from her."

Next problem to solve was smuggling the bottles onto the air base without getting caught. Only officers — not enlisted men — were allowed to have liquor on the base. "We had an empty B-4 bag (canvas garment luggage) and we filled it up with the bottles. As I carried the bag, you could hear all the bottles clinking together," Doyle recounted. They took the bag onto a bus going back to the base and took seats way in the back. When it was time to get off the bus, Doyle stayed in his seat until Dick could take the bag from him through the window. They caught an open air tram back to the rest area, and Dick jumped off while the vehicle was slowing to a halt, and when it stopped Doyle handed the bottles to Dick without arousing suspicion. Mission accomplished! They had enough liquor for the glorious celebration that would come sooner than expected.

Inevitably, the Jeter Crew's time at rest came to an end on April 29, 1945. In his log, Dale Henderson described the 35-day break as "the best time ever spent in the Army."

CHAPTER 8: BACK TO THE WORK OF WAR

On May 1, 1945, the Jeter boys were back on Guam, and on May 9, they flew another bombing mission to Truk. It was their 24th with 13 more to go. The boys had come back to their digs at Guam from a beautiful month on Oahu and plunged right back into battle with missions to Marcus and Truk, both treacherous targets. Of the Marcus mission over Moen Island, Henderson wrote: "First mission since rest. The kind we like, no flak. All kinds of planes were over the target, P-51s, P-47s, B-29s, B-17s, and B-24s. Good bombing, (Greg) Babykin laid them in again."

The mission to Truk on May 13 was not so smooth. Years after the war, Henderson wrote a complete account of this flight where they almost "mushed in" (crashed). He gives credit to Frank Jeter and co-pilot Herb Harter for keeping an underpowered takeoff from turning into a disaster. On this Sunday morning in May, the crew was scheduled for a bombing mission to Truk. The Jeeter Bug had been red-lined due to engine problems so the Jeter Crew was taking Sweet Routine, which was also not in good mechanical repair. Weighted down with 3,200 extra gallons of fuel and five 1,000-lb bombs in the bay, Sweet Routine was slowed down by her poorly performing No. 3 engine.

John Weller recalled that the ground crew chief had also red-lined Sweet Routine that day, but the maintenance chief overruled him. "He was told to fly everything that day! The ground chief told Frank to go gentle on No. 3 engine, not to push it." Weller explained: "Supply lines were not plentiful once you got beyond the Hawaiian Islands. You made do with replacement airplane equipment by cannibalizing aircraft that was no longer flyable. The ground crews did a masterful job of keeping our planes in the best condition they could with the parts they had."

Getting off the 5,000-foot long runway of Harmon Field was always a challenge because the extra 2,000 feet past its end was covered with stumps of cleared trees. Henderson, the Jeter Crew radio man destined to become a historian, had a talent for great story telling. He remembered the details—and the emotions—of the team's most harrowing experiences, and he wrote them down. "More than one of our planes got into trouble on takeoff and didn't make it, crashing into those damn stumps and exploding," Henderson wrote. After the clearing there was heavy jungle for about three miles and then an army hospital in a direct line with the runway.

"On takeoffs, I sat at my radio and watched the right wheel leave the runway," Henderson wrote. "Just as the wheel left the ground, No. 3 engine blew and oil covered it. I grabbed Larson, our engineer, by the arm and pointed. He took one look and yelled to Frank we had lost No. 3. We were beyond the point of no return so Frank pushed all engines. He kept #3 going until we were up and over the clearing. After getting every little bit of power out of it, Herb feathered the engine. We were starting to lose air speed but couldn't salvo the bombs until we cleared the hospital.

"When we finally did, Herb pulled the salvo lever. The draft that hit the bomb bay slowed us even more. We were down to 89 mph, at or below stalling speed, when the bombs let go. It was as if something had kicked the old girl in the fanny. She took off and we went back around and landed. I, for one, got out and rolled and hugged the ground.

"How Frank and Herb kept that plane in the air I'll never know. They got every bit out of those engines that was possible. I do know that we were not more than a second or two from mushing in," Henderson wrote. Sixty-five years later, Weller recalled: "We never found those bombs."

Heading into June of 1945, the Jeter Crew members were getting ready to move to Okinawa for the next chapter of their war story. Called upon to ferry people and materiel to Okinawa from Guam, the crew had an experience that again left Dale Henderson shaken and happy to get back on the ground.

Henderson on another episode: "high speed stall" on June 11, 1945. The crew, minus the gunners and bombardier, was returning to Guam after a ferry mission to Okinawa. Henderson sets the stage with a description of the B-24's good points *and* its bad points.

"The B-24 was a great airplane," he began. "Compared to the B-17 it could fly faster, further and carry a heavier load. It did have one very bad characteristic. It was prone to high speed stalls. More than once, as its pilot was buzzing the field the plane continued right into the ground, killing all aboard."

Needless to say Henderson was concerned when he realized the Jeeter Bug was dropping suddenly on approach to Harmon Field on Guam. "On landings, (Bob) Larson, our engineer, went below to check the nose gear, and I stood between the pilots to call out the air speed. As we approached Harmon Field, we were doing about 250 mph and were at about 1,000 feet. Frank (Jeter, the pilot) started to pull back on the wheel and then hit Herb (Harter, co-pilot) on the arm, and they both were pulling back but nothing was happening. We were down to 800 feet and were now doing 275 mph.

"The next thing I knew they both had their legs braced and were straining to pull back the wheel. Still we settled down to 600 feet and the air speed was up to 290. Suddenly Frank let go of the wheel with his right hand and hit the trim tab wheel. It spun to 9; the nose of the "Bug" came up and she started to climb."

Perhaps what happens next is typical of a man like Frank Jeter who seemed to "fly" through life with aplomb, confidence and "cool." Henderson relates: Frank looked over at Herb and grinned. He turned to me and simply said, 'high speed stall.' It might have been nothing to him, but to me that hard ground was getting very close *fast*."

As stress was building for crews on Guam, drinking too much on their off time and participating in reckless behavior was not uncommon. John Weller tells the story of a B-24 navigator nick-named "Pic" whose friends intervened to save him from what seemed like certain death or court martial. "By this time (June 1945), most of our squadron had completed 27 combat missions. Some men were becoming combat weary. Everyone was needed, as replacements were not coming on a regular basis. This is a true story of how a man was put back on track by his fellow airmen and a thoughtful flight surgeon:

"Recreation was limited for all personnel in combat areas. Our main form of relaxation after a mission was to partake of whatever liquid refreshment was available—beer or booze. This navigator had the habit of taking whatever vehicle was available, even the CO's jeep and driving around the island. So far he hadn't been injured or wrecked a vehicle, but it was only a matter of time that he would be caught or wreck a truck or jeep. Our flight surgeon had an idea: We would make sure Pic had a lot to drink. Once he passed out the doc put him in a plaster cast from the waist up, including one shoulder and arm.

"When Pic woke up, our story—and we all stuck to it—was that he had taken the CO's jeep and drove it into a palm tree. The power of suggestion was great because he said he was in pain and asked us to wait on him hand and foot, and we went along with it. Eventually, though, he caught on to what really happened and demanded to see the doctor to tell him off. That didn't work too well, though, because the doctor reminded him that he was the only one who could remove the cast and free Pic from bondage. So they made peace, and this crude method of therapy worked. The flight surgeon removed the cast, and Pic never stole another vehicle."

Six weeks after the boys almost bought it on Sweet Routine, a fellow 26th Bomb Squad crew, well known by the Jeter boys, had the misfortune of drawing the same ship for their fated mission on June 26, 1945. The plane was still not performing well. The Paul Farnham crew relived the horror of the Jeter Crew's salvaged underpowered takeoff from Guam. But theirs was not a happy ending.

Sweet Routine crashed off the runway in the same treacherous location Dale Henderson described in his recounting of the Jeter Crew's close call on May 13. Luckily, the Jeter boys weren't scheduled for a mission that day so they didn't witness the fiery crash that killed their friends. Seven crew members were killed; incredibly the gunners and radar operator got out of the inferno.

Doyle Ebel remembered the group as "Rogers' crew," for engineer William J. Rogers, the one he knew the best. Also killed were pilot Farnham, bombardier William A. Bloom, co-pilot C. S. Needles, navigator Norman Truscott, radio operator F.W. Krause, and assistant engineer E. DiCarlo. Surviving were radar operator D.S. Handy, aerial gunners William J. Hoeltge, Bernard Gapinski and L. H. Thibault. The Jeter Crew did the honors at the Farnham Crew's funeral and burial on Guam.

When they started out to war the Jeter boys knew there would be danger. And along the way they surely had their brushes with catastrophe. But they were convinced that nothing terrible would happen to them. That's what they had been trained to think, and having that attitude was extremely helpful in avoiding panic, stupid mistakes and unnecessary risks. So Frank Jeter's crew had cohesiveness, mutual respect and a bit of bravado to keep them going.

In some ways, they may have been denying their fear of death. They went about their job with a certain sense of duty and confidence, even though uncertainty, exploding and burning B-24s and airmen meeting their deaths were all around them, if they chose to acknowledge it. But they didn't.

Doyle Ebel recalled: "You didn't think about that. The only time you thought about it, you know, is when you would be in your tent there and realize that the day before across the tent from you there'd been a bunch of guys you knew, and the next day they wouldn't be there and it would bring you to the reality that it could happen."

John Weller put it another way: "We just concentrated on what we had to do. It was like there was nothing else you could think about. The rest of the world seemed out of focus. We were in our own kind of world."

Farnham's crash wasn't the first tragedy on a takeoff from Guam. There were many others. Death was all around. An earlier 11th Bombardment Group crash on takeoff from Guam was a preview of what happened to Farnham's crew and what could have happened to the Jeter Crew. A B-24 called "Ball of Fire" became just that on the same runway on March 20, 1945. 2nd Lt. Arthur Leitz of the 431st Bomb Squad was piloting the aircraft on a night harassment mission to Chi Chi Jima when it lost power as he was trying to take flight. Witnesses said the lights on "Ball of Fire" went out momentarily and then came back on. The plane climbed sharply and then swerved to the left. Witnesses then heard a "swish" sound as the craft hit the trees about a half mile off the runway. The plane then disappeared behind the trees and witnesses said they saw a flash and heard an explosion.

All men on the crew lost their lives that day. They were: pilot Leitz, co-pilot Laurence T. Fuglaar, Jr., navigator George P. Scroogy, Jr., bombardier Earl A. Swanson, engineer Ralph C. Curry, assistant engineer Alexander Yowko, radio operator Hugh S. McCall, Jr., radar operator Joseph C. Skoozypies, and armorer/gunners Martin J. Kenefake, Jr., John C. Miller, Jr., and Kesler W. Harbin.

The "Norman B. Mackie" crew, trying to take off for a mission to Marcus, suffered a similar fate. 2nd Lt. Paul E. Moon of the 494th Bombardment Group was flying the B-24 (44-41497) when it crashed and burned May 1, 1945, on the runway at Harmon Field, Guam. 1st Lt. Charles E. Wilcoxon witnessed what he called the "crack-up" of Moon's plane: "I was sitting at the end of the runway when the ship started. About half or two-thirds of the way down the runway the plane swerved to the right, and blue smoke came from either No. 3 engine or the right tire. From where I was it looked as if the right tire might have blown out. We could see then they were trying to stop, but couldn't, and ran off the end of the strip. As it went off, fire was coming from it. Immediately it seemed to be engulfed in fire, and a series of explosions started a few moments later."

Moon and the rest of the 10-man crew were all lost: co-pilot Frank J. Lark, navigator Irving M. Stein, bombardier Bernard Miller, engineer James C. Rich, Jr., radio operator Arthur Dobrow, upper turret gunner Edward Dalrymple, nose gunner Hiram Craig, ball gunner Paul K. Rosar and tail gunner Charles L. Dugger. The plane was named for a member of a different crew. Norman B. Mackie was not on board when the ship crashed.

On May 8, 1945, 1ˢᵗ Lt. John Lowe of the 98ᵗʰ Bomb Squad, also part of the 11ᵗʰ Bomb Group, was pilot on a bombing mission from Guam to Marcus. Lowe's plane "Temptation" was the last over the target, and his No. 4 engine caught an anti-aircraft shell before the crew could drop their bombs. On the return to Guam, the plane was losing fuel and losing power as darkness came. Lowe, who had 38 of his requisite 40 missions, decided to ditch in the sea about 70 miles northeast of Saipan.

All but two of the crew were buried at sea. The survivors, navigator 2ⁿᵈ. Lt. Harold Vigue and Cpl. Raymond De Roo were rescued by a Navy PBY and returned to duty. Vigue was awarded the rare Soldier's Medal for his heroism in helping to evacuate the crew from the plane. De Roo, interviewed in a video posted on YouTube, said after the entire crew landed in the water, Vigue had pulled him aboard a life raft. De Roo said for his part in the flight he was pinned with a Purple Heart while recovering in the hospital. He returned to duty on May 27; Vigue came back on July 14. De Roo said he didn't see his friend Vigue again until after the war when he visited him at home in Maine.

On June 19, 1945, Floyd W. Beanblossom led a B-24 crew whose fate was bound up in a lot of confusion and one crew member's misplaced and tragic heroism. Beanblossom, of the 42ⁿᵈ Bomb Squadron, 11ᵗʰ Bombardment Group, took off from Guam for Marcus with 1ˢᵗ Lt. Robert C. Davis as co-pilot. The No. 2 engine was hit over the target and the plane was losing altitude after the bomb run. The damaged engine wouldn't feather and was leaking fuel. Via radio, the Navy's rescue unit Dumbo advised Beanblossom to "land" on the sea and to do it before dark. Beanblossom's crew realized they couldn't make it back to Guam and, according to witnesses, the pilot began circling and decided the crew should bail out, which 10 of them did at 6:40 p.m. The engineer, TSgt. Guillermo Abrego, however, decided to stay on board and to fly the plane to Tinian on his own. He crash landed on Tinian's West Field #2 at 2 a.m. and was severely injured and died several hours later. The rest of the crew was picked up by a submarine later that day; all who bailed had survived except Sgt. John F. Barrett, a gunner.

For co-pilot Robert C. Davis, surviving this flight was his second great stroke of luck in this horrible and cruel war. Davis' plane had spontaneously exploded and was disintegrated by fire on the runway at Johnston Island back on October 21, 1944; the crews of the 42nd Squadron were getting ready to take off for Guam on the second leg of their flight from training on Oahu to the Pacific war front for the first time. Minor repairs on his plane, #939, on the layover had apparently resulted in a fuel leak that caused the combustion and destruction of the plane and its contents.

Capt. S. Sherley, historical officer, writes in the October 1944 42nd Squadron monthly report: "The route down was to stop the first night at Johnston Island, the next at Kwajalein and reach Guam on the third. Lt. R. C. Davis's airplane met with disaster at Johnston on the 21st. While undergoing minor repairs in the morning prior to takeoff, fuel which had leaked into the bomb bay section was ignited, it is believed, by a short circuit of the wires in the transfer system. Squadron navigation maps and all the records and correspondence of the Ordnance Department were aboard the airplane, not to mention the personal belongings of the crew and passengers, three cases of beer, three crates of fresh eggs and 600 pounds of potatoes." Amazingly nobody was injured in the explosion.

While war was raging on islands closer to Japan, life could go on somewhat peacefully in secured areas like Guam. At times insulated from the noisy, smoky and smelly battles, air crews and the native residents experienced episodes of calm, and *good things* actually happened. Such was the case with Whitey Whiteside, a navigator with another B-24 crew.

In the midst of relative serenity, Whiteside, half drunk, stumbled one night into a wonderful and unforgettable experience on Guam. John Weller tells the story: As Whitey and a buddy were driving in a jeep back to camp after some serious partying, they were waved down by a native Chamorro on the road. The man told Whitey that his wife was in labor and he needed someone to fetch her mid-wife and bring her to their home.

Whitey got sober in a hurry as the father-to-be and his buddy took off in the jeep and left him to tend to the laboring mother. Before the dad could get back with the mid-wife, the baby was born with Whitey's unrehearsed delivery skills. "She gave birth with Whitey's 'help'—he did everything she told him to do." Mother and baby were fine and the mid-wife took over for Whitey. Quite amazed at his apparent competence, Whitey told Weller: "I never delivered a baby before!"

The family of the newborn was grateful for the help the boys had given, and they invited them to the child's baptism celebration, a huge deal in the Chamorro culture. When it came time to decide what to call the baby, the parents deviated a bit from tradition and gave him a name that honored Whiteside: John White White. Who knows if the name stuck? Presumably, the parents gave their baby boy another more traditional Chamorro name as well.

Despite frequent leveling of rank in an army of men risking their lives for their country, some clung to protocol, even in the war zone. Weller recalled: "(At first) the officers of the Jeter Crew were invited to frequent the U. S. Navy's main officers club on Guam to enjoy a drink. The Navy officers came in dress whites; we came in whatever we could find to wear. After a couple of visits we were told by our commanding officer that (someone of the Navy brass had complained and) we were no longer welcome at their club. I guess that we were considered to not be gentlemen!"

CHAPTER 9: REST OF THE STORY, OKINAWA AND THE END OF WAR

The eyes of the world were on the Pacific War as summer began in 1945. The war that had devastated Europe was finally over. Hitler and the Nazis had been crushed and were no longer threatening to take over the Western world. Americans were jubilant but had their reservations — Emperor Hirohito and the Japanese military were still hanging on despite the Allies steady and sure progress toward Tokyo. The Japanese promised to fight to the last man and to kill any and all American sailors, marines, soldiers and airmen who came within their grasp before the emperor's fighting men drew their last gasp. The horror facing the Jeter Crew that June was virtually indescribable.

Missions were suspended at the end of June so the 26th Squadron could move to the newly taken island of Okinawa, their next home base. From here they would begin to strike at the Japanese home islands and Japanese-held areas of China. By now, the 20th Air Force had brought the full power of its hundreds of B-29 bombers to bear on Japanese cities, relentlessly firebombing urban targets every night.

While still on Guam, Frank Jeter selected John Weller to attend a special code writing school to learn language skills that might be needed if any of the crew's upcoming missions over China or Japan went sour. Weller was to learn to write letters home in code. Luckily, these skills were never needed, much to Weller's relief. "This proved to be a very difficult assignment," he recalled.

Weller also felt fortunate never to have to bail out over enemy-held territory. In pondering a question about training for how to bail out and handle a parachute, Weller recalled. "We were never given any instructions. We were just told, 'count to 10 and pull the rip cord!'

"Before our raids into China, each crew member was given two flags," Weller recalled, "an American flag with information as to who we were written in different languages and a Chinese flag that had Chinese script with a personal 'chop' number (for identification) for each flyer. The flag carried the message: "I am a downed American airman. I have come to help rid your country of our common enemy, the Japanese. If you keep me safe, provide me with food, water, shelter, and medical help, you will be rewarded by my government when I am returned safely to my countrymen" (The U.S. Allied Forces)."

Before each raid, Weller was issued $8,000 to $10,000 in Chinese currency — enough for the entire crew if they had to bail out. Upon the crew's safe return, the money was returned to Army coffers.

"We were told that if we had to bail out in a remote area we would probably be taken to the nearest village leader and be forced to follow his instructions, even if they went against our customs or morals. If we didn't do as we were told, the leader might turn us over to the Japanese! Thank goodness we didn't have bail out!"

The Jeter Crew joined in many of the myriad and massive air raids, along with the bombers and fighters of the Navy, Army, Air Corps, and Marines. They shared the makeshift island home with the flyers of the 20th and the revered B-29s, as well as with the fighter groups that continued to pound Japanese targets. Okinawa was covered with runways to accommodate the comings and goings of hundreds of war planes bent on bringing down the empire and ending the constant carnage.

The Pacific Ocean was alive and smoking with every weapon and vehicle the United States had been able to muster for the years of war production that began with Pearl Harbor in late 1941. The Allies outnumbered the Japanese in vehicles, weapons and men. From the American point of view, this lingering catastrophe had to end. But the proud underdog was not giving up.

Unbeknownst to most Americans, including the Jeter boys, the Allies would soon have a new weapon of unimaginable power that would bring the nightmare of World War II to an end with a huge bang. The secret weapon — the result of a frantic scientific quest to harness nuclear power — was being brought to the

Pacific in parts to be assembled on Tinian in the Mariana Islands near Guam. Combatants in the Pacific were hoping and praying the Japanese would surrender before the Allies were forced to invade the Japan home islands, but there were few signs of that happening.

Meanwhile, the Jeter boys were intensely aware that their lives were in grave danger as every new day dawned on Okinawa. Would they run out of luck before they finished their 40th and last mission? By the time they got to Okinawa, they had completed 27 missions. They'd beaten the odds on their Iwo Jima misadventure in March before getting their month of rest. The ultimate question was: will they get to go home — and when? These young warriors knew survival wasn't assured. They'd seen their buddies die and they could only hope and pray that their fate would be different.

Like Dale Henderson, tail gunner Doyle Ebel is a great raconteur. But Ebel doesn't write his stories down; he tells them, often regaling his audience with the humor as well as the drama of the events. Ebel allows that the "high speed stall" and other close calls like the May 13, 1945 "underpowered Guam takeoff" episode were "kinda hairy." However, he adds in his best Houston dialect: "that wasn't the hairiest part I've ever done," giving him the entre to relate what for him was the most frightening of them all.

It was on a return flight from the July 15 mission to Usa, Japan, when armorer Sam Tillery alerted Ebel that all the bombs hadn't dropped and that there might be a live bomb still in the bomb bay. "Well, he came back (from checking the bomb bay) and stuck his head through the door and said: 'I need some help in here.' So I went down there with him."

What the two 21-year-olds discovered were two bombs that had dropped from upper racks and landed on the lower racks and failed to drop out over target. One in particular had been armed when the wind that swept through the bomb bay had unscrewed its impeller and rendered it live and ready to go off at any second.

"There's a catwalk down through the bomb bay," Ebel explained. "It's about 10 inches wide. Over on the other side of the airplane there was a piece of channel, an aluminum channel.

It had an angled iron deal that stuck out about two inches over there. So Sam and I straddled that bomb bay with one foot on the catwalk and one foot on the other side outside with the bomb bay doors open.

"We're 8,000 feet up there looking straight down," Ebel relates. "Sam is back there and he is pushing and easing that bomb towards me, real careful like cause this thing is ready to go. So we take it out and finally I got it in my arms. And I just dropped it down through the bomb bay. On the other one the arming vane hadn't come off of it yet, so we secured it and dropped it. Then we just toggled the others out and got rid of all of them.

"(Since that day) I've always thought about it. We didn't have any parachutes or anything on, either. We couldn't work with them on. It wouldn't have done any good anyway. We would have been down in the middle of the Pacific Ocean. To this day, I think about it and (realize) all that plane had to do was hit an air pocket or something and shift a bit and it would shift both of us right out of that bomb bay!

"(In later years) Sam asked me one time: 'Doyle do you ever think about that?' I said, 'Yes, I think about it all the time. Now I get cold chills when I think about it.' And he said: 'Me too. I didn't realize it at the time, but do you know or realize what could have happened to us.' And I said: 'Yes, I do.' We didn't even get an honorable mention. We should have gotten a medal." This episode hasn't been written up before by anyone, neither Doyle, nor Sam, nor Dale or John.

One day in July, when nerves were frayed from 30-plus bombing missions, Frank Jeter and John Weller tempted fate one night on Okinawa, their last island assignment. "We'd been drinking together and we ran out of booze," said John. "I don't know why but for some reason we thought we needed more. It was strange because we *never* got into each other's belongings. But we went into Greg's personal things and started drinking from a special bottle of Russian liquor he was saving.

"We had a couple of pours from his bottle, and while we were drinking them, Greg came back into the tent and caught us. He

91

was furious. He said, 'I'm going to kill you!' and grabbed his .45 and threatened to shoot us. "We had to convince Greg that shooting us with a .45 was not the right thing to do.

"We finally got him calmed down and he agreed not to shoot us," John remembered with a smile. But it took many years for Greg to ever forgive John and Frank for their transgression.

On July 17, 1945, the Jeter Crew joined a big raid on the largest airfield in China, Chiang Wan in the Shanghai area. This was the first mission to China for the Jeter boys but overcast kept them from seeing the ground. They joined many other 7th Air Force squads that included B-24s of the 494th Bomb Group (Kelley's Cobras), B-25s, A-26s, P-47s and P-51s. Two 494th B-24s were hit over the target.

"Sitting' Pretty," piloted by Lt. Harold H. Eifler of the 494th, took a direct hit that knocked out the No. 1 engine and damaged Nos. 2 and 3 just after bombs away. "About 10 seconds after I saw our bombs drop there was a terrific blast, wrote tail gunner John P. Stukas. "I saw a flash and a column of brown smoke just under our ship. Before I knew what had happened, my tail guns were knocked into my lap. Engineer Raymond P. Lasko added: "All the glass was knocked out of the nose, injuring the bombardier (Keith C. Haws). There were three holes 6-inches in diameter and many more small ones in the main fuel cells. The armorer gunner Marion E. Thackston, Jr., was slightly injured by flak that shot out the elevator trim tab cables."

Tail gunner Stukas continued: "Before bailing out, I saw gasoline coming into the waist (center section of the aircraft) like heavy rain, and the escape hatch was flown up with a flak hole in it. The plane was losing altitude. After I bailed out, I saw the plane go into a steady dive and crash on one of the islands near Shanghai."

All members of Eifler's crew bailed out and six members were rescued by friendly Chinese guerilla forces and taken back to Okinawa a few days later on a Chinese junk. Pilot Eifler, co-pilot Darwin R. Dively, navigator William R. Martin, Jr., and nose gunner Clyde J. Sellers were captured by the Japanese when they reached the ground. Dively tried to escape and was shot on the spot by Japanese soldiers. Eifler, Martin and Sellers were released from a POW (prisoner of war) camp at the end of the war and returned home. Other airmen on Sittin' Pretty that day were: radio operator James R. Lee, Jr., and ball turret gunner Buford L. Hughes.

Crash of the second 494th B-24, piloted by Lt. William L. Trowbridge, was equally dramatic. Over the target, the name-less lead plane took a direct hit and there was an explosion of one of the bombs just after the load was released. The force and heat of the blow-up were felt by crew members of other aircraft in the formation. Pilot Trowbridge later described the damage: "All four main gas tanks were badly leaking. The hydraulic sys-tem was completely destroyed. The whole bomb bay was badly mangled. Both wings had numerous holes so that they looked like sieves. There was a very large hole by the radar spinner and the spinner had been knocked out." Trowbridge and crew realized quickly that the plane would not make it back to home base and made the same judgment the Jeter boys made when they were in trouble. "At that point we decided not to attempt a ditching. Ditching of that plane would have been 100 percent unsuccess-ful," Trowbridge wrote.

Before giving up the ship, the crew tried to resurrect one of the engines when the fuel tanks inexplicably stopped leaking for a short time. There was hope for a few minutes that the rejuve-nated engine would get them back to base. But then No. 1 and 2 engines both ran out of gas and No. 4 was on empty as well. "This happened above 6,000 feet. The crew was signaled and told to bail out. I was the eleventh man to jump, followed only by Major William E. Gernert, the command pilot of the formation. When I broke through the overcast, I saw 10 chutes in the air and hitting the water. I also saw the spot where the plane went into the water. It was a flaming mass of oil and gasoline."

While waiting for the pilot's order to "hit the silk," several crew members noticed that ball turret gunner Fred Cianfrini had his chute on upside down. When they turned it over, they saw it had been hit by flak and was useless. Luckily, nose gunner

Arthur T. Stanford had packed a spare chute, which he gave to Cianfrini. Stanford described the bail-out experience: "When I hit the water and discarded my chute, I had lost all sense of direction. I wanted to go with somebody, but was unable to see anyone at first.

"Finally I saw a head bob up about 200 yards to my right so I started to swim toward it when I heard Cianfrini call my name. I knew he didn't know how to swim so I struck out for him. I found I wasn't getting anywhere with my Mae West (inflated floating vest) so I took it off and was by his side in no time. I held on to the neck of my Mae West and Fred hung on to the other end. We gave up hope of being picked up that night, so I put my Mae West back on and Fred rode piggy back until the next morning. At day light, we thought we saw an island and started swimming to it. After about two hours of that, we noticed Dumbo coming over the horizon."

Of Trowbridge's 12 crew members who bailed out, seven were rescued after being in the drink for 20-plus hours. The other five: radar operator Richard F. Anderson, engineer Robert R. Holder, radio man James D. Mitchell, upper turret gunner Charles E. Brown, Jr., and tail gunner Norvell A. Cain didn't survive the ocean and were listed as killed in action. When the search in shark-infested water for the lost five was called off, Commander Gernert wrote: "I believe it reasonable to assume that those five members met death in the water due to causes unknown. In my 20 hours in the water, I did not see another member of the crew." The other surviving crew members were: co-pilot William A. Yosburg, navigator Carl A. Ogrine, and bombardier Joseph D. Sorden.

The Jeter Crew joined in another raid on the same target on July 22. This time they could see the Chinese landscape clearly. Of the raid Henderson wrote: "Really gave it (the target) a plastering. Saw China, very green and very low. Saw muddy waters of the Yangtse (River). The 494th and B-25s went in first. Watched gunfire, fighters strafed, knocked out some (planes on the ground). Bombs started large fires."

At this stage, things were getting more and more intense. On July 25 the Jeter Crew took off from Okinawa on a mission to Kikai Shima, along with the 494th. Dale reported in his log that he was given the order to abort and the 11th Bomb Group turned back. But the 494th went on, even though the fighter escorts hadn't been able to get off the ground due to the weather.

The 494th bombers got jumped by 20-30 Zekes (Japanese fighters) over the target and lost a B-24, Kuuipo (sweetheart in Hawaiian), piloted by Lt. John C. Anderson. Kuuipo was hit by two Japanese fighters about three minutes after leaving the target. Fellow pilot Odell E. Stone saw the B-24 get hit with about 20 anti-aircraft shells that blew a hole 2-feet square on the right rudder control surface. Stone said the No. 2 gas tank was also hit and began spraying fuel. Almost immediately, Anderson radioed that he had a fire on the flight deck and he was going to order the crew to bail out. A short time later, however, he changed his mind because the crew had gotten the fire under control and he thought he could make it back to base.

The weather was bad—they passed through three storm fronts on the return flight—so the pilots were having trouble keeping the planes together. Stone said Anderson was keeping up with the others and radioed that he was doing fine and was going to make it. "It was two hours and 18 minutes after he was hit that he exploded," Stone said, "and during this time we had radio contact with him. At 1400 I called and asked him if he thought he could make it. He said yes, so I told the radio operator to contact the base and inform them that the damaged aircraft would make it home. About 10 minutes later while we were flying in the soup, he exploded. He gave us no warning."

Pilot Marvin C. Smith, flying on Anderson's left wing about 100 yards to the rear and side of him, saw the explosion. "Shortly after we broke out of the third front Lt. Anderson's ship exploded with the left wing falling off. It fell in flames and disintegrated in the air, with the right wing also coming off right after. We swung left to circle and when I came in sight again I saw two chutes low and six chutes at 5,000 feet. We spiraled down as soon as they were all in the water and we flew in low at 100 feet and dropped two five-man life rafts, one single-man life raft, radio, supplies, etc."

Smith radioed in the coordinates to the rescue team and because they were running low on fuel left the crash site for base. "We counted seven men three different times as we passed over," Smith reported. The Air Rescue Unit picked up engineer Charles D. McLaughlin and nose gunner Elliot J. Deutsch later but called off the search the next day. The rest of the crew was never found.

Killed in the crash of *Kuuipo* were: pilot Anderson, co-pilot Andrew J. Lohneis, navigator Joseph J. Gjondla, bombardier Bruno J. Mariotti, radio operator Waldo M. Keeney, waist gunner Orlando L. Webb, ball gunner Marion F. Bandur, tail gunner Eugene M. Linn, and radar operator Albert E. Shiposki. According to Dale's log, Anderson's crew was on their 39th mission with only one more to go before they could go home. *Kuuipo* had also seen a lot of action; she had completed 45 combat missions before her demise.

On July 28, the 494th took off from Okinawa for Kure Harbor on Honshu, Japan, with the intention of sinking the Japanese Battleship *Haruna*. Two B-24 crews were shot down in that failed raid. Both *Lonesome Lady*, piloted by 2nd Lt. Thomas C. Cartwright, and *Taloa*, piloted by 1st Lt. Joseph Dubinski, were hit by anti-aircraft fire just after dropping their bombs: *Lonesome Lady* crashed at 12:48 p.m. and *Taloa* hit the ground at 12:51 p.m.

Cartwright, one of only a few who survived, wrote many years later: "In quick succession my plane was hit, but we could still fly. I did not realize how badly we were damaged and planned to head for the open sea where there was hope that our Naval seaplanes would spot us and pick us up if we ditched and survived. We started losing altitude and the controls were becoming less responsive and I could not head out to sea — the plane flew back toward land on its own. Although not burning, the B-24 went into a vertical dive into overcast and crashed into a rice paddy outside of Hiroshima near the village of Ikachi.

"All of the crew were able to bail out and were scattered for miles along an area south of Kure Harbor in a mostly wooded, sparsely populated area. We were all captured and after some harassment taken to a city (he later learned was Hiroshima). We were always blindfolded when out of a prison cell. I saw all of our crew there except navigator Roy "Pete" Pedersen and Bill Abel, the tail gunner." Cartwright, who was moved to a POW camp in Tokyo for intense interrogation, later found out that six of Lonesome Lady's crew members were still interned at Hiroshima on August 6, 1945, and were killed by the blast of the first Allied atomic bomb, "Little Boy." Pedersen, whose parachute didn't open properly, died when he hit the ground in the dense forest near a remote village, and tail gunner Abel survived as a prisoner in a camp at Kure.

Killed in the atomic blast were: co-pilot Durden W. Looper, bombardier James M. Ryan, radio operator Hugh Atkinson, engineer Buford J. Ellison, nose turret gunner John A. Long, Jr., and ball turret gunner Ralph J. Neal. Postwar, the remains of Atkinson, Looper, Neal, Ellison and Ryan were recovered and transported to the United States.

The fate of the Taloa crew rivaled that of the Lonesome Lady in its horror and gruesomeness. After being hit by ack ack, the plane made a slight turn to the left and then went into a steep dive. Witnesses saw it burning on the ground near Yawata village. Co-pilot Rudolph C. Flanagin was thrown out of the plane through a huge hole blown out by flak, and he landed at the mouth of a river near Hiroshima. Engineer Walter Piskor was also ejected from the plane and dropped to earth unrestrained, landing on the roof of a Mitsubishi shipyard factory.

Four of the Taloa crew members -- pilot Joseph Dubinski, navigator Lawrence A. Falls, top gunner Charles R. Allison and nose gunner Camillous F. Kirkpatrick—died in the B-24. Commander Donald F. Marvin, bombardier Robert C. Johnston, radio operator David A. Bushfield, lower gunner Charles O. Baumgartner, and tail gunner Julius Molnar got out of the plane and were taken prisoner by the Japanese. Baumgartner and Molnar were in a Hiroshima POW camp on August 6 and died when the atomic bomb hit. Bushfield and Marvin died in a Japanese prison. Bombardier Johnston, interned in Tokyo, was the only Taloa crew man to survive to the end of the war and go home. The remains of Baumgartner and Molnar were recovered postwar and were shipped to the United States and buried at Jefferson Barracks National Cemetery.

On July 29, the Jeter Crew joined the 494th on a second mission to Kure Harbor to sink the Haruna. This time the raiding party included hundreds of warplanes from the 7th and 14th Air Force units, and from the U.S. Navy. The target ship was found in the harbor, where most of the surviving Japanese fleet was docked.

Dale Henderson wrote in his log, "We flew up the strait between Kyushu and Shikoku islands. (It was a) maximum effort. (There) must have been 1,000 planes in the air. Heavy flak, not accurate, much of it colored (red, green and orange) from different (Japanese) ships so (their) gunners could gauge accuracy."[5] The mission was successful and the Haruna was sunk.

Dale continued in his log: "All participants claimed a hit. So much action, impossible to give credit to any one plane. The Navy will probably get the credit. A big show, clear day." Dale also noted that the skies were filled with Corsair fighters on attack duty, strafing a crippled Japanese cruiser as the Jeter Crew made its way back to Okinawa. (In the end, the Navy gave credit to the 11th Bombardment Group, which included the 26th Squadron, John Weller added as a postscript.)

At the beginning of the war, Dale Henderson wrote in his diary that he didn't want to be a war hero. But 12 days before the war ended, he insisted on going above the call. On July 30, 1945, on Yontan Air Field on Okinawa, Dale instinctively ran up to a shot-up B-24 to help recover the body of a dead nose gunner. Four other members of the Jeter Crew, Doyle Ebel, Dick David, Sam Tillery and Ray Fritter, were with Henderson on the airstrip

---

5 Many years later, John Weller met Navy torpedo bomber pilot Charles Stroeher who flew off the USS Franklin Aircraft Carrier in the same attack of Kure Harbor on July 29, 1945. "We were talking about our war time experiences, and Charles said: 'I've got to tell you about the time the Japanese used colored flak. No one thinks this happened,' " John related. "I told him: 'Charlie, I had the same reaction. We must have been on the same target at the same time.' "

cleaning their guns when the B-24 crash landed. Doyle urged Dale not to go, but Dale wouldn't listen. He had to take action. When warning was given that the B-24 was going to blow, the rest of the crew took refuge behind a huge pile of rocks, Doyle said.

While Dale was close to the B-24 on the shoulder of the runway, a Navy fighter taking off from the busy airfield blew a tire and crashed into the B-24 that had three fused 500-pound bombs on board. With the collision, the bombs exploded and both aircraft burst into flames. The fighter (probably a F6F-5 Hellcat or a F4U-1 Corsair) was carrying an exterior-mounted cylindrical tank of fuel, which exploded into flames and began rolling down the runway in Dale's direction. He tried to outrun it but was caught by the tumbling inferno. He was severely burned over most of his body.

Dale downplayed the horrific accident in three sentences in his memoirs: ". . . I was injured in an airplane accident. Twenty-three were killed and only two of us survived. Because of the accident I was not discharged from the Air Corps until August 16, 1946."

Doyle fills in the blanks: "They took him to the hospital on Okinawa. I visited him there and he was all covered in bandages with only his lips showing . . . He had a lot of plastic surgery. They had to reconstruct his left ear. They did a lot of skin grafts on his hands and back. The damage was mostly from the waist up." Later Dale was treated at the hospital on Guam and eventually transferred to Tripler Army Medical Center in Honolulu. Ultimately, he didn't look the same as before but Doyle says "He was still the same Dale he always was."

Dale's injuries landed him in intensive care and rehabilitation for almost two years. Even though he could have died from his burns, he was not eligible for a Purple Heart because his injuries were not sustained in actual combat.

Keeping the log for 32 successful missions, Dale had to relinquish his recording duties to John Weller and Doyle Ebel for the balance of the war. The rest of the Jeter Crew technically still had eight more missions to go, unless the stakes went higher and they were asked to do more than 40. Or, they could get lucky and the war would end before they reached 40. The 26th Squadron continued to fly missions from Okinawa to strategic targets on the islands of Japan. They flew another mission to Kyushu, Japan, along with the 494th Bomb Group on July 31. The boys encountered heavy and accurate flak on their foray to Sasebo naval port but made it back safely to Okinawa.

Sadly, not everyone on the Sasebo raid made it back without incident. Pilot Weldon Dyess and fellow crews of the 98th Squadron had been diverted from another mission to bomb the entrance of an underwater tunnel on Honshu. Bad weather forced a change in plans and Dyess's crew and four others aimed for the Sasebo-Nagasaki port target.

Dyess's plane was hit over the target, and he radioed the others that he was going down. Before bailing out, he tried to contact "Playmate 34" of the Navy Dumbo rescue service. Two other pilots, Lt. Oren Kinsey and James Brown, heard Dyess's call for help but they didn't hear the rescue crew's answer. The next day, a rescue submarine crew reported seeing four life rafts and six to 10 survivors in the distance near the area where Dyess went down. But the crew was never found.

The eight members of the Dyess crew were reported missing in action. They were: 1st Lt. Dyess, co-pilot 2nd Lt. Robert Studer; navigator 2nd Lt. Nathaniel Hoffman; bombardier 2nd Lt. Serge S. Davison; 2nd Lt. Charles S. Ensey, an observer; engineer Sgt. Aubrey B. Dixon; radio operator Sgt. Orval D Moore; and gunner Cpl. Lester A. Kuhnau.

Later the news came out that six of the Dyess' crew and observer Ensey were taken captive and executed by the Japanese. Sgt. Moore died in the crash.

On August 5, 1945, the Jeter Crew was back in the air over Tarumizi, a large agricultural area on Kyushu. They dropped a dozen 500-pound fire cluster bombs and then let go of leaflets urging the Japanese people to surrender. The leaflets reported that the Russians had joined the Allies' battle against Japan, and there was no hope for a Japanese victory. A plane flying above the Jeeter Bug dropped an entire bundle of leaflets that hit the plane with great force, shattering the top turret. Pieces of debris hit radar operator Dick David on the head, knocking him out briefly but not hurting him seriously. The next day, August 6, 1945, a B-29 bomber commanded by Paul Tibbetts, flew over Hiroshima and dropped "Little Boy," the first atomic bomb ever used in combat. This attack, which killed about 70,000 people, should have changed the game. But the Japanese were still not ready to give up.

On August 7, the relentless enemy was waiting for the formation of B-24 bombers that showed up over Kyushu to bomb an industrial center at Omuto, 38 miles northeast of Nagasaki. While the Jeter Crew let go of their eight 1,000 pound bombs, they encountered heavy flak but didn't get hit. The crew of a bomber piloted by 1st Lt. John Morgan of the 431st Bomb Squad wasn't so fortunate. Morgan's ship was right next to the Jeter Crew over the target.

Before they could drop their bombs, Morgan's crew was hit in the bomb bay by flak and burst into an inferno. From the tail, Jeter Crew gunner Doyle Ebel saw the flash from about 100 feet away. As the plane fell apart and dropped to the sea, Doyle glimpsed one man attached to a parachute and thought he may have seen two more that were too far below to make out. But the news wasn't good: Morgan and the rest of the 10-member crew were all killed that day in the explosion above the home islands of Japan.

On August 9, three days after the dropping of the atomic bomb on Hiroshima, the crew could see the residue of the explosion on a mission to the port city of Iwakuni, Honshu, which is 22 miles southwest of Hiroshima. "The air is still dirty and smoky (at 12,000 to 14,000 feet)," John Weller wrote in the log. He adds in later writings: "On our return to Okinawa, we were told to stay at least 50 miles east of the Nagasaki area. We had no knowledge that an atomic bomb was to be dropped on Kokura or the alternative target, Nagasaki. A few minutes after 11 a.m., I observed a cloud of smoke rising from the Nagasaki area. It kept rising above 25,000 feet. On the log Weller wrote: We reported a large fire and that a major target had been hit. The mushrooming cloud reached high altitude. (We) knew damage was extensive."

On Saturday, August 11, the Jeter boys woke up early to fly

another mission to Kyushu. They carried a dozen 500-pound fire clusters in their bomb bay, which they dropped on Kurume, a railway and manufacturing center 50 miles northeast of Nagasaki. They encountered fighters and accurate flak over their target but once again dodged any devastating blows. Little did they know that when they landed back on Okinawa that day after a total of 336 combat hours and 37 missions, they were finished with this hellish war that had robbed them of their innocence. Who knew that they were finally done dropping bombs and risking their lives over Japan and that they could go home to resume a normal existence?

It was Sunday morning, Aug. 12, 1945, when the Jeter Crew loaded up their airship with fragmentation bombs and taxied out to the runway for another bomb run over Japan. They were surprised and thrilled when a jeep driver from headquarters chased them down and turned them around with the message: "War is over!" As John wrote on the log: "Taxied back and CELEBRATED!"

A day or two later, they flew an anticlimactic mission over Japan—with no bombs—to make sure the Japanese were honoring the armistice the Allies had negotiated to bring the war to an end. "Did not encounter anti-aircraft or resistance. Instructed not to take offensive. Carried ammo, but no bombs. Flying time 6:00," read final entry in the flight log.

CHAPTER 10: MAKING OF THE "JEETER BUG"
DOCUMENTARY

In 1945, when the Jeter boys were unknowingly living through the most consequential time of their lives, technology was rudimentary, to say the least. At home, Americans were driving big lumbering cars and hanging our clothes on a line in the backyard to dry. We had no microwave ovens, no television, no stereophonic sound, no compact discs, no world wide web, and certainly no digital cameras! We typed on typewriters, read books and listened to the radio. We made our meals from scratch, and we sat next to our neighbors and friends at Saturday night showings at the local movie theater. Thongs were a type of almost-barefoot shoe, and over-the-fence chats were more common than cross-country or even cross-town telephone conversations.

The application of emerging science to develop more sophisticated ways of fighting a global war made victory possible. The U.S. harnessed new technology to use radar to detect the enemy's approach to battle. Computers were put to work to decipher coded enemy messages; government labs made penicillin to give the wounded a chance to survive on the battleground; and the government put the heat on scientists to hurry up and manufacture an atomic bomb. These same advances paved the way for a brave new technological world in America.

The Cold War space race, consumer insatiability, and affluence have driven a colossal mushrooming of convenience products that we don't think we can live without in 2013. They've also spawned technological advancements that have taken us to the moon, to develop satellite and telescope systems that allow us to see into our universe's vast and incomprehensible past, and to realize our own insignificance.

As primitive as visual arts may have been in the 1940s, consumer devices to record life in motion did exist. Filming equipment that used "film," not tape, not computer chips, not even electronics, was available, and Frank Jeter picked one up to take to war. He chose the light weight (1½ pounds) and compact (6 ¼" X 3 ¾" X 1 ⅔) Keystone Model K-8 movie camera. Presumably, he also took a supply of film for the hand-held, wind-up camera that shot 8mm. What *was* he thinking? If he didn't already know, he must have soon found out that filming the war wasn't allowed! The military wouldn't even allow servicemen to keep diaries or talk about their experiences in letters home. We'll never know all the scenes Frank chose to film; most of the reels were confiscated and never made it past the censors.

Nevertheless, Frank Jeter kept his camera among his wartime possessions. It was easy to carry. It was small and compact. The view finder on the side folded flush with the body when not in use. You didn't need batteries. You just wound it up. The key on the side, like that on the back of a wind-up doll, was easy to turn and also folded down for compactness. Frank passed the camera around and encouraged all his crew to take a turn filming their activities. Sometimes they were just fooling around and having a good time. Other times were dead serious, like the time they were dazed and confused on Iwo Jima eating breakfast on the morning after their emergency landing. Other times they were getting their craft ready for a mission, warming it up, turning the propellers. In retrospect, they were recording their phenomenal luck. Many a B-24 blew up inexplicably on the runway while crews were getting ready to takeoff. They even filmed China from the air on a mission to Shanghai. The film is extra grainy and flickers a lot, but the cameraman got a pretty good view of a B-24 known as Night Mission, whose crew later crashed over Kyushu, Japan.

After the war, Frank Jeter went home to Texas with the miscellaneous canisters of undeveloped exposed film that had escaped the censors. He threw them in the back of a closet and forgot about them. Years later, the crew's unofficial historian, Dale Henderson, remembered about the film and asked Frank to find it. Frank's discovery of the home movies set into motion a decade-long saga of bringing the film to light and leveraging it to tell the fantastic and virtually untold story of the American aviators in the Pacific who risked their lives almost daily to do their part to win the war.

With modern technology, the canned film could be brought to life, first on VHS tape, and then on DVD (digital video disk), cleaned up and enhanced digitally and brought to 21st century American audiences via public television.

The Jeter story gets new life in 2002 when two men — navigator John Weller and NBC cameraman Charles V. Sullivan, Jr., — meet completely by accident at a health club in San Jose, California. Sullivan is lost and asking for directions, and John Weller is helping a stranger find his way to an ice skating rink (Direct Logic). They began to chat and it didn't take long for Weller to touch on the Jeeter Bug war story. When he mentioned the 8mm footage from the war front, he got Sullivan's attention. Retired from filming documentaries for NBC, Sullivan was married to Linda Sullivan, the president of NBC 11, the local affiliate of the national commercial network.

John Weller, bursting with a 60-year-old story he was dying to tell, realized when he met Sullivan that the Jeter Crew possessed something rare in that old resurrected Keystone footage. The vintage film could illuminate for new generations the wartime daily lives of B-24 crews fighting the Pacific war, and specifically highlight the Jeter Crew's courageous and incredible drive to stay alive to tell the story. "You have something no one else has," Sullivan told Weller. "This is very valuable. We have to do something with this." He talked to his wife about his find, and she confirmed his instincts that the film should be shown somehow. Weller showed him the footage and the documentary became a project. Sullivan agreed to help Weller find a producer.

Enter Grace Provenzano, seasoned television reporter and newscaster and associate professor of broadcast journalism at San Jose State University (an associate professor at San Francisco State University since 2006). Sullivan made the connection for Weller, and Weller went to see Grace in her office with the VHS tape in hand. He showed her the footage and recounted the Jeter Crew story. Interested, Grace said she would like to do a project with the film, perhaps for the History Channel or PBS. What happened next is amusing due to its ironical twist. Weller, thinking "I'm not turning this over to just anyone," asked to see

Grace's resume. So she showed him. He was impressed and not just a little embarrassed.

Grace Marie Provenzano started her career in television news in 1986, and when she met Weller had 15 years' experience as a reporter/newscaster for various big media enterprises, including CNN, United Press International Radio in London and Deutsche Welle International TV in Berlin. She covered the fall of the Berlin Wall for Deutsche Welle and reported post-Iron Curtain stories in Europe for the award-winning PBS program "European Journal" in the 1990s. She has a Master's of Mass Communications degree from Arizona State University and taught journalism courses there for five years. She did graduate work as a Rotary Scholar at the University of Kent in England and attended the University of Vienna in Austria, also doing graduate work. She also earned a bachelor of science degree in Social Sciences at Michigan State University and has won many awards for her reporting, including first place in the Arizona Press Women competition for a TV special on climate change in the Phoenix metropolitan area ("The Heat Is On," 1998).

As an added bonus, Grace had a personal as well as professional interest in World War II and international politics. Her uncle served in Europe and her mother had been a "Rosie" working in a Detroit war production factory. Grace had covered the 50th anniversary of the end of the war while in Europe in 1995 and was glad to be able to make the "Jeeter Bug" documentary that would be aired in 2005, the 60th anniversary of the Allied victory.

Needless to say, Grace seemed to be the right person to take on the "Jeeter Bug" documentary. Her initial challenge was to find sponsors for project funding. She got a Junior Faculty Grant from San Jose State University in 2003 for pre-production and another from the California State University system in 2004 to complete production. She also found a friend in PBS. "I went to PBS in San Mateo and said: 'I think I have something here." Having produced documentaries for a PBS station, KAET-TV in Phoenix, she was familiar with the types of stories public television might want to produce. Passionate about the project, Grace kept in touch with PBS and began digging up more information, photos and film assets to demonstrate the documentary's value.

She was successful in getting PBS on board with the project, and Josh Springer of KSCM public television was assigned as Grace's co-writer and supervising producer. Grace also recruited her husband John Cannon, a former national sportscaster, as associate producer and narrator. Springer was a producer for KCSM, which was at that time associated with the College of San Mateo. One of Springer's first steps was to call John Weller in to the station to learn more about the "Jeeter Bug" story and to pin down the authenticity of the details.

"I learned in a hurry that a PBS documentary has to be backed up by facts," Weller recalled, who had become project researcher, along with Charles Sullivan. "There can be no fiction, that is, no unverified information. I don't want to say he 'grilled' me but at one point he asked if he could play the devil's advocate to be sure everything we were talking about was factual." Weller told Springer that he and his son Jim had searched for independent witnesses who saw the Jeter Crew's emergency landing on Iwo Jima more than 50 years before. Their search, including Jim attending the Third Marine Division Association reunion in Scottsdale, Arizona, in 2004, had been fruitful. At the reunion, Jim found 1st Sgt. Marine John Farritor who remembered the craft bumping down the Japanese runway at 3 in the morning March 13, 1945. Farritor flew up to San Jose from Oceanside, California, and was interviewed in his full dress uniform for a supplemental clip to be distributed along with the documentary.

In the spring of 2003, six of the seven surviving Jeter Crew members and their wives traveled from their homes in Texas, California, Hawaii and New York to the D-Day Museum in New Orleans. The impressive and expanding WWII museum was the perfect setting for Grace to interview each of them on camera about their war experience for the documentary production. While in New Orleans, the "Jeeter Bug" crew members were presented with a "Road to Victory" certificate signed by Stephen Ambrose, renowned WWII historian/writer and founder of the museum, for their forced landing on Iwo Jima. They also took a tour of the exhibits with Grace, an experience she says she will hold in her memory forever. "Walking through with these gentle-men and hearing their stories really brought the artifacts to life," she recalled. "The 'Jeeter Bug' crew experienced the war together and it was wonderful listening to them explain what it means to them. I've always looked up to their generation, my parents' generation. They went to war; they did what they were told to do; they were selfless, and when they came home they had been changed. They would never be the same."

Grace's personal enthusiasm about documenting the "Jeeter Bug" story made her tenacious about getting the film made despite any obstacles. "I stayed on it for two years, spending my time outside of work editing and writing," she recalled. She col-lected many photos from the crew members and their families and arranged to have them videotaped to add to the film's visual richness. The local PBS staff helped her find supplemental war footage and to acquire audio that represented how the air war actually sounded. "At a certain point they (KCSM) offered to help complete the post-production 'in-kind' because of the high cost of completing the project on my own," Grace said.

The documentary "The Jeeter Bug: Mission over Iwo Jima" premiered on February 8, 2005, at the Louis B. Mayer Theatre at Santa Clara University. Six of the crew members and marine John Farritor traveled to San Jose for the public showing and gala that followed. For Grace, it was a professional and personal triumph, the result of hundreds of hours engaged in a labor of love. In her opening remarks, she revealed that she and her husband were not only excited about the debut of the film but also because it was their first night out after adopting twin girls from Russia two months earlier.

T.J. Holmes of NBC 11 in San Jose interviewed Weller about the documentary, and the station carried a report about the "Jeeter Bug" on its evening broadcast the night after the premiere, includ-ing clips from the film. The documentary, accepted by PBS for national distribution in late 2004, airs annually on many PBS sta-tions throughout the country around Memorial Day and Veterans' Day. The film was shown at the Poppy Jasper Film Festival in November of 2005 and as producer Grace garnered the Broadcast

Education Association Award of Excellence in April of 2005.

After the initial airing, Weller received a letter from Herbert Karner of Broken Arrow, Oklahoma, another marine who was on Iwo Jima when the Jeter Crew landed. Karner wrote of his personal reaction to the film that brought the battle for Iwo Jima back into his consciousness. "Because the marines I have visited with say they know of your visit to Iwo confirms my suspicion that the passage of time does funny things with memories. In fact, a lot of things I am now seeing and hearing make me wonder if I really was there, and if my experiences are nothing more than a bad dream."

Co-pilot Herb Harter's videographer son Dave immortalized the premiere event by creating a DVD showing the audience, the speeches, the after party and, later at Weller's home, Doyle Ebel's regaling of the crew and families with his many war stories. John Weller took advantage of the frivolity to again seek absolution after all these years for his and Frank Jeter's indiscretion in stealing Greg Babykin's prized liquor one day back in 1945.

"Every time I saw Greg after the war, at all the reunions, I would always bring him the best bottle of bourbon I could buy and I'd ask him, "Greg, do you forgive me for drinking from your bottle?' and he always said in a gruff voice, 'No, I *do not* forgive you.'

"But finally in 2005, at the premiere of the 'Jeeter Bug' documentary, I asked him again, 'Greg, can you forgive me now?' and he said, 'Yes, I forgive you.'"

Waimea Falls, Oahu, as the Jeter Crew saw it in 1945. Note the guys at the top. *Photo courtesy of the Jeter Crew.*

Dick David, radar operator, and Doyle Ebel, tail gunner, on Oahu for rest and recreation. *Photo courtesy of the Jeter Crew.*

The remnants of a festive champagne-fueled 22nd birthday party for Dick David on Oahu during rest, April 23, 1945. *Photo courtesy of the Jeter Crew.*

Waimea Falls swimming hole on Oahu, April 1945. The boys had to cut their way to this remote spot through the jungle. Pictured here are: Jeter Crew member Sam Tillery, third from left, and members of the Otto Schultz Crew, including Donald Olsen, fifth from the left, and Schultz to Sam's right. *Photos courtesy of the Jeter Crew.*

Dr. and Mrs. Gordon Lightner, hosts to Weller and Harter on Maui during R&R, April 1945.

Dale Henderson and Ray Fritter on Waikiki Beach, Oahu, 1945

The Jeter Crew did the honors at graveside services for members of Paul Farnham's crew who were killed in a crash on takeoff from Guam in Sweet Routine. Farnham, bombardier William A. Bloom, co-pilot C. S. Needles, navigator Norman Truscott, radio operator F.W. Krause, and assistant engineer E. DiCarlo died in the crash. *Photos courtesy of the Jeter Crew.*

Air Force map of the Pacific Theater July 1945 as the Allies get close to Japan.

A 21-gun salute for the fallen aviators of Paul Farnham's crew, Guam, June 1945.

View of the American cemetery on Guam, 1945. *Photos courtesy of the Jeter Crew.*

Jeter Crew mission over tiny Marcus.

Jeter Crew's bombing of Marcus, March 24, 1945. *Photos courtesy of the Jeter Crew.*

The Jeter Crew on Okinawa: Front row, Doyle Ebel, Dick David, Bob
Larson, Ray Fritter, Sam Tillery and Victor Crowell; back row, John Weller,
Greg Babykin, Herb Harter and Frank Jeter. Missing is Dale Henderson,
who was badly burned in a airfield crash late July 1945.

Co-pilot Herb
Harter, left,
with Pilot
Frank Jeter.
*Photos
courtesy of the
Jeter Crew.*

Kuuipo, one of the 494th Bomb Group's B-24s, on the runway. Kelley's Cobras flew many missions from Okinawa with the Jeter Crew. Kuuipo, piloted by Lt. John C. Anderson, went down July 25, 1945 over Kikai Shima.

The Japanese battleship Haruna under attack in Kure Harbor, Japan. *U.S. Air Force photos.*

117

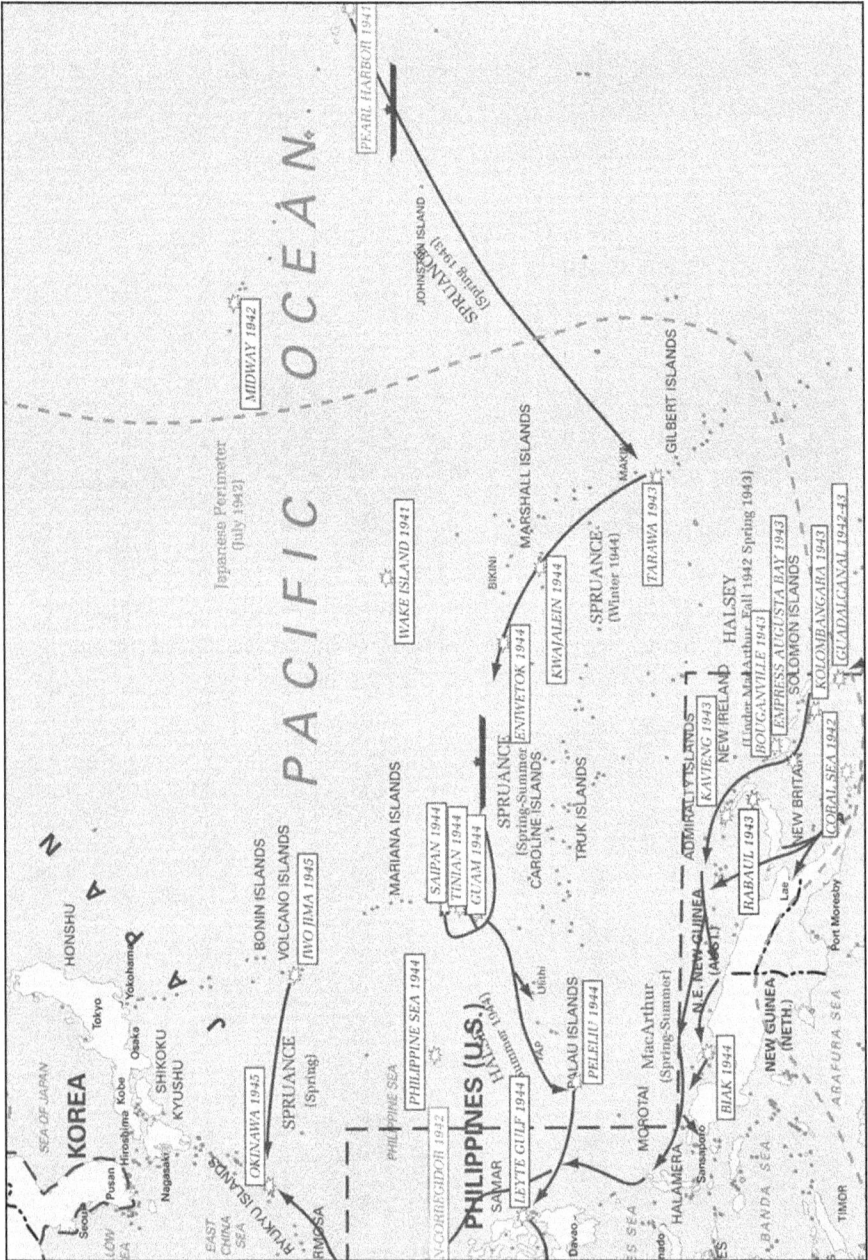

U.S. Air Force map showing the Allied Forces' "island hopping" across the Pacific Theater from Guadalcanal in 1942 to victory over Japan in August 1945.

Returning from a mission to Iwakuni , Japan, on August 9, 1945, the Jeter Crew caught sight of the second atomic blast, which devastated Nagasaki, Japan. *U. S. Air Force photo.*

感激
の
握
手

EMOTIONAL HANDSHAKE

The Soviet entry into the war against Japan means that at last Japan is now in the hopeless predicament of having to take on the armies of the whole world. You already know well the ending of that crack German army that tried to blitz through Russia and of the leader of that stampeding tactic, the militarist Hitler. It must be a fact deeply etched in your minds that, having faced the counter-attack by the Soviet army, the master of Eastern Europe, all of the Germany army on the eastern front have been wiped out.

In a hard fight over several years, the Soviet army has accomplished the great deed of conquering the Germany army. Now that the fighting in the European theatre is over, the Soviet army has replenished and rebuilt itself above and beyond the prewar level both in quality and qualtity. At last, the Soviets are joining the united front against Japan.

The road that should be taken by Japan, now that the allied powers are ready to advance on all fronts against Japan, and now that Japan's inevitable and wholesale destruction is about to begin. . .

You all know well, too, what that only road is that will save your beautiful homeland Japan from miserable war and destruction!

Reproduction of the pamphlet U.S. flyers dropped over Japan, August 1945. John Weller arranged for the original document written in Japanese to be translated into English by Tetsuya Kataoka, senior research fellow (now retired), the Hoover Institution at Stanford University. *Images courtesy of John Weller.*

In 1979, Herb Harter, at far right, and John Weller, second from right, met a pair of marines who recalled the Jeter Crew's landing on Iwo Jima in 1945. The chance meeting was in Colorado where the veterans were attending their respective military reunions. John kicked himself later for not getting the marines' names. *Photo courtesy of the Jeter Crew.*

1979 11th Bomb Group reunion, Denver. Posing in front of a van with a "Jeeter Bug" replica are: front row from left, Ray Fritter, Greg Babykin, Frank Jeter, Dale Henderson; back row, Herb Harter, John Weller, Dick David and Doyle Ebel. *Photo courtesy the Jeter Crew wives.*

Above, unidentified anti-aircraft artillery gunner on Iwo Jima facing Motoyama Airfield, No.1, the runway the Jeter Crew landed on during a firefight in the wee hours of March 13, 1945. *U.S. Air Force photo.*

At right is Marine 1st. Sgt. John Farritor, who manned such a gun on the night the Jeter Crew flew in. Jim Weller, John Weller's son, tracked Farritor down and his first-hand account was documented in the "Jeeter Bug" film project in 2005. *Photo courtesy of John Farritor.*

Catholic Mass in Denver, 1979. Front row, Jackie David, Pattye Ebel, Jo Weller, Dale Henderson, Fr. Chris (Ray) Fritter (who said the Mass for the group) and Roberta Harter; back row, Dick David, Bernice Henderson, Herb Harter, John Weller, unidentified Dominican priest, Doyle Ebel and Greg Babykin.

At left, "The Jeeter Bug" documentary creator Grace Provenzano and Jeter Crew navigator and film instigator John Weller, at the premiere of the documentary, 2005. Weller presented Grace with a plaque declaring her an honorary member of the "Jeeter Bug" crew. *Photos courtesy of the Jeter Crew.*

123

Part 2

The lives and times of the Jeter Crew members after the war is won

CHAPTER 11: FRANK JETER, PILOT

Frank Jeter had to grow up in a hurry. His father died of leukemia in 1940 when Frank was 17, forcing him to quit high school and take over the family's tile setting and floor covering business. Frank married Mary Ruth Burkhart the same year, and in 1941 the couple's first child was born.

A picture of his adorable two-year-old Marsha Lee hung in Jeter's tent when he and his flight crew were flying bombing missions over the Pacific Ocean. By 1944, Jeter already had a second child, William Frank Jeter III, who was born in September of 1944, just after the Jeter Crew finished two months of Bomber Command advanced training in Kahuku, Oahu, and before reporting to Hickam Field for gunnery training.

Frank Jeter's life story in 1944: breadwinner, business owner, husband and father at 17; U.S. Army Air Corps cadet at 19; twin-engine pilot at 20; B-24 four-engine pilot at 21; father of two; pilot and flight commander of an 11-man B-24 bombing crew at 22.

Becoming a pilot was Jeter's passion, and he was relentless in his pursuit of it. He joined the Army on Aug. 24, 1942, a few months after his 19th birthday. He was told he wouldn't be accepted to the academy without a high school diploma. But he passed the written examination and was accepted for Air Corps cadet training.

He completed his basic training at Polaris Flight Academy in Lancaster, California, and took his advanced training with the 312th Twin Engine Flight Training Group in Marfa, Texas. He graduated in January of 1944, received his wings and rose to the rank of 2nd Lieutenant. Frank received his four-engine pilot training at Kirtland Field in Albuquerque, New Mexico, to qualify as a B-24 pilot. His first assignment was to assemble a B-24 crew at Hammer Field in Fresno, California, in April 1944.

In looks and manner, Frank Jeter was the quintessential rugged World War II pilot. He wore his weathered leather bomber jacket and Air Force cap with pride and carried himself like a hero. He was handsome and sported a slight moustache and aviator shades. When the crew was shipped to the Pacific Theater, it was Jeter's idea to bring along a camera to film the war. His personal Keystone Model K8 was the instrument the Jeter Crew passed around to record the highlights and routine moments of their war experience.

In lighter moments on the plane, Jeter mugged the camera and gave a wink and a smile as if he were Humphrey Bogart or someone equally debonair. He smoked cigarettes and cigars and seemed to thoroughly enjoy his time at war. He never showed fear and instilled confidence in the men on his crew. By all accounts, he knew what to do and had the respect and affection of his men. He trusted them and they trusted him.

There are two things Frank's crew members remember vividly about him: one, that he was a great leader and pilot; and two, that he drank a lot. Radio man Dale Henderson's first impressions of Frank were recorded in his diary June 27, 1944, having met Frank about two months before: "I've never seen anyone drink more (than Frank) except my stepfather."

Harter deadpanned: "Frank had a tendency to drink a little once in a while. He liked to know that we all could hold our liquor. That was all part of it." Harter quickly added: "But he never drank while we were flying, and he did a good job of taking care of the rest of us." Tail gunner Doyle Ebel said of Jeter: "He was a brilliant pilot because he could handle situations, and he did look out for his crew. Nobody ran over us while Frank was around."

Initially, at least one crew member found Jeter difficult to warm up to. Radio operator Dale Henderson wrote in his diary in 1944: "I can't figure Lt. Jeter out after over two months. He's a damn good pilot but he wants to keep a distance between him and his officers and the enlisted men." That standoffishness appears to have completely evaporated by the end of the war. In his memoirs, Henderson said of Jeter: Frank was a great guy. He was a leader."

When the Jeter Crew went their separate ways after 37 combat missions, Frank Jeter went back to Dallas, Texas, where his wife and two children awaited his return. He picked up the flooring business where he left off and made a success of it. In 1954, he joined forces with Robert Millar and launched Jeter-Millar, Inc.

He and Mary Ruth were divorced in 1963, and Jeter remarried in 1969. His new wife, Ginger, joined him in the business and helped him turn it into a multi-million dollar venture that included contracts with Dallas Public Schools, and school districts in Oklahoma and New Mexico, as well as big office buildings in downtown Dallas and Fort Worth.

In 1975, Millar retired and sold his half of the business to Jeter's son, William Frank Jeter III, who goes by Bill. Jeter and his son were partners for five years, and according to Bill they "had a great time and made a lot of money." In 1980, they split the business and Bill launched his own company, Bill Jeter, Inc. [6]

In 1985, Bill brought his daughter, Jenny, into the business, and Frank helped to train her. Meanwhile in 1979, Dale Henderson had contacted all the members of the Jeter Crew and insisted they come to Denver to a reunion of the 11th Bombardment Group, which included their bomb squadron, the 26th. Everyone came to the reunion and when the group got together in Jeter's hotel room they each brought one or two bottles of liquor. "The dresser looked like a bar," recalled John Weller with a laugh.

While catching up with Henderson, Frank Jeter revealed that the forgotten reels of film from the war were buried in one of his closets at home. Henderson, a history buff who fondly remembered his war buddies and their exploits, was adamant that Jeter must resurrect the film.

Sadly, by the time the film was discovered by a documentarian with the interest and juice to bring the story to the public, Frank Jeter had already died of leukemia in 1989 at the age of 66. His consolation was that he was reunited with his buddies and got to relive their shared experiences both in person and in the films, which Henderson had converted to VHS for all the crew members.

6   Construction News, Dallas-Fort Worth, June, 2005.

Over the next ten years, Frank Jeter saw his war buddies at the reunions. The Jeters and Hendersons even shared a vacation to Disney World in Florida in 1987 with the Hendersons following the Jeters home to Dallas for a visit. "Frank proudly showed us around the Dallas-Fort Worth area and the many skyscrapers where he had the contract to do the flooring and tile work."

When Frank died in 1989, many of the Jeter Crew members were in the Dallas area for the 50th anniversary of the B-24 Liberator. Despite the sadness of the occasion, the guys were glad they could show their respect and affection by serving as pallbearers at Frank Jeter's funeral.

CHAPTER 12: JOHN WELLER, NAVIGATOR

You can't really talk about John Weller without including his wife of 58 years, Jo Corbett Weller. John is a kind and gentle man who came back from the horrors of war with the intention of putting his combat experience behind him. He was largely successful because he found a compatible partner who focused on the good things life had to offer. John's young life had been interrupted by a war that abruptly sent him to face the rigors of combat — and the constant threat of death — in the ultra-bloody Pacific Theater. Jo also had her war scars.

Though she was safe at home during the war years, Jo suffered one of the cruelest wounds. She lost her older brother, Larry, who had doted on his baby sister and made her a treasured toy car out of wood. He had also helped her to build a dollhouse and furniture when she was a young girl. Raised on a small farm in North Platte, Nebraska, Jo was acutely aware of the troop trains that went through her hometown every day carrying boy warriors on their way to battle. Her community's women famously threw themselves whole hog into giving the boys the royal treatment for 15 minutes on their stop in North Platte.

Ernest John Weller (he prefers his middle name) was born to Ernest A. Weller and Lillian Bleifus Weller in Hollister, California, on May 1, 1923. John lost his mother at the age of three and his father remarried. The family moved to San Jose where John attended San Jose High School. He distinguished himself in high school as an enterprising advertising salesman for the school paper, the *San Jose Herald*. For this success, he won a trophy for keeping the paper solvent. He graduated from high school in 1941 and enrolled in San Jose State College as a pre-med student in the fall, just months before Pearl Harbor.

Weller was in the backyard of his parents' home in San Jose, California, when he heard that the Japanese had bombed Pearl

Harbor and Hickam Field on the island of Oahu. At that time he could never have predicted how intimately he would come to know Oahu and its environs over the next five years.

Anticipating the draft, Weller enlisted in the Army Air Corps in March of 1942, having been told he could finish his education before going to war. All bets were off in early 1943 when the Army abruptly ordered him to Wichita Falls, Texas, for basic training for the cadet program. It was a shock for Weller who at 19 had never been away from home. He recalls boarding a troop train in Oakland, California, and two days later arriving at Wichita Falls. "I was in a new world where my life was to change. I'd never experienced sleeping with 24 other guys and being told when to get up to go to the bathroom and when to eat and sleep. I learned to follow orders and to do what I was told to do," he said.

After basic training, Weller landed at Texas A&M University for flight-related classes. He was also being tested for skills needed to be an airman. The program included training with civilian pilots who assessed a cadet's aptitude for becoming a pilot. Weller vividly recalls one experience with a pilot trainer named Temple Smalley.

"I will always remember him (Smalley) for one particular training in flight," Weller said. "After five hours of instruction he told me to take the plane up to 5,000 or 6,000 feet and do a power-off 2 ½ spin. I replied: 'Yes sir!' We went up and I stalled the plane out and started in the spin. About a turn and a half down, my hand hit the throttle! We did get down on the ground alright. I got us out of that mess. When we landed Mr. Smalley said to me: 'I'd like to talk to you Mr. Weller.'

"I said 'okay, but can I go to the latrine first?' I was sure that when I came back I was going to get dressed down, but instead he surprised me by saying he thought I would make a good pilot! I told him right away I didn't want to fly; I wanted to be a navigator. Fortunately, the air corps was looking for navigators with ability in science and math to take courses to learn navigation."

From then on navigation would be Weller's passion and his crucial role on the Jeter Crew. He took his navigation training at San Marcos, Texas, graduating in Class 44-3 in March 1943. After a short leave, he reported to Hammer Field near Fresno, California, where he joined the Frank Jeter Crew and started advanced training to fly a B-24 heavy bomber. "I met the men I was going to spend the next year and a half with. I would trust my life to them, as well as their trusting me."

During their deployment to the air war in the Pacific, the Jeter Crew dutifully bombed their targets and rarely saw the effects of their missions. But while on Iwo Jima after their emergency landing, young Weller saw more of the carnage than he had ever expected. "I asked one of the Marine officers if he would take me on a tour of the island," recalled Weller. "We took a jeep over the hill to the battlefields, and I saw dead bodies stacked up like cord wood. I told the officer 'get me the hell out of here' after about two minutes. We could hear the flame throwers that made a kind of whooshing sound. As a flyboy, I'd never seen anything like it before."

After V-J Day when the Jeter Crew was dissolved and the men went home, Weller made his way to San Jose, California, his home town, as it turns out, for life. Shortly after he got home, Weller received a call from Jim Haigh's mother in Los Angeles who asked to come and visit him in San Jose. "She knew her son had been killed and wanted to talk about it," John related. "I told her as much as I could, mostly about the good times we had." As many war veterans did after they came home, Weller eased Jim's mother's pain by filling in details of her lost son's war experience and the circumstances of his death. He did the same for the bereaved family of Paul Farnham, who was killed on Guam. John went to see Paul's parents in Campbell, California, which is close to San Jose.

Once settled, John went to work for his father at Sunshine Bottling Company in San Jose and made plans to go back to college. The medical career abandoned, Weller enrolled at Stanford University as a junior in March of 1946. He graduated with a bachelor of arts degree in economics, and to nurture his navigation/star gazing passion, a minor in astronomy.

Following his June 1947 graduation from Stanford, Weller

started his career with Crown Zellerbach Corporation in September. That move turned out to be a fortuitous one, and Weller enjoyed a 37-year career with the paper company. He rose through the ranks over the years to managing positions in Marketing, Sales and Account Management. The last six years of his career gave him a chance to step back and enjoy the fruits of his labor as the company's ambassador to major clients.

In 1952, Weller met Jo Corbett, who by then had become a Californian. She had come out to California in 1949 with her sister Ginger and her family and settled in the Bay Area. She almost got scared back to Nebraska by a California earthquake, but decided ultimately to stay to enjoy the state's beauty despite the dangers. John and Jo married in 1953 and settled in San Jose. Before long they began to have sons. The first boy, William, came in 1957; the second, John, followed in 1959; James was born in 1963. John and Jo bought their first house in the San Jose neighborhood of Willow Glen and have lived there for over 50 years. They expanded and updated several times to make the small house into a comfortable home for a family of five.

In many ways, the Weller family has lived a traditional American life with Sunday dinners and frequent family camping trips. Their granddaughter Emily describes their life: "The family would pack up the old station wagon and head to the mountains for a week of hiking and fishing. Jo kept alive for the family the tradition of Sunday dinners she had enjoyed as a girl on the Nebraska farm. Many Sundays were spent attending mass at St. Christopher's (Catholic Church in San Jose) where the boys also attended school, then gathering with the family for a fabulous home cooked meal."

The Wellers have four grandchildren: Emily and Benjamin, children of son John, and Katy and David, children of son William.

Life wasn't always so sweet and nice for John, however. When he first got home from the war, he had trouble getting onto an airplane. "I didn't fly for 10 years," he relates. "I finally forced myself to get on a commercial plane because I was in business. I had to." Today he speculates his fear had to do with his lack of control. Weller also admits he had to seek professional help when his war demons got the better of him. The first time was when he was still a student at Stanford. He sought help again in recent years. "I got help. I feel bad for the guys who didn't."

As a navigator, John felt tremendous responsibility for his fellow airmen. "You had to be perfect. You had to be in complete control and later when I had three boys, I think I might have moved my need for perfection onto my boys. I am thankful I married Jo. She understood me. In 57 years, she has never pressured me because she knew what I was going through." John also acknowledges that there were times after the war when he was drinking. Alcohol had become a justifiable habit during wartime. It was a comfortable and convenient way to temporarily escape the tragedies and turmoil of combat.

One way for Weller to relieve residual war stress has been to meet with his war buddies and catch up on their postwar lives. Throughout the years, the Wellers have helped to organize Jeter Crew reunions where they have gotten to know one another's wives and children well. John says getting back together with the crew sparked his and others' interest in documenting their stories. They still keep in touch with the remaining crew members and with the families of those who have died.

When John retired in 1986 he began a new adventure as a volunteer. For three years he worked as a staff volunteer in Congressman Tom Campbell's office in San Jose. Campbell asked him to serve on the committee to interview prospective candidates for the Air Force Academy and West Point. The committee's job was to recommend the best individuals to Campbell for academy appointments. "This was a great experience for me to meet some of the finest young people and learn how much they had accomplished in just a few years. We can be very proud of the cadets in our academies," John said.

Former Congressman Campbell wrote Weller a note after the release of the "Jeeter Bug" story in 2005: "Congratulations! I'm so happy that the story of your Iwo Jima landing, rescue of the (aircraft) and unbelievable courage will now be told on television. It was such an honor to work with you the years we had together; and knowing more now of your military service to our country, I'm glad you exercised the authority you did in connection with the military academy appointments. It's a real honor to know you John."

Tom Campbell represented the San Jose/Silicon Valley area in the U.S. House of Representatives from 1989 to 1993 and 1995 to 2001 and the California State Senate from 1993 to 1995. Campbell was a professor of law at Stanford University in the 1980s and 1990s and the dean of UC Berkeley's Haas School of Business from 2002 to 2004. He served as the state's finance director under Gov. Arnold Schwarzenegger from 2004 to 2005. In 2011, he was appointed dean at Chapman School of Law in Orange, California.

CHAPTER 13: ANATOLE "GREG" BABYKIN, BOMBARDIER

Jeter Crew bombardier Anatole "Greg" Babykin came to America with his White Russian parents when he was an infant. His parents, both soldiers in the counter-revolutionary Russian Army, had barely escaped with their lives as the victorious Bolshevik regime took over their country.

In 1921, Gregory John and Tatiana Babykin traveled with the retreating army across the Black Sea to Constantinople (Istanbul today) where they turned in their weapons and were granted asylum by the Turkish government. On the way, Tatiana led a group of stranded school children across the Caucasus Mountains to the Turkish border on foot. For this feat, Tatiana, only 16 at the time, was awarded the Cross of St. George, one of Russia's highest military honors.

Tatiana had run away from home at 14 and disguised herself as a man to join the army supporting the provisional government during the Russian Civil War. She served as a frontrunner for the unit commanded by her uncle who was a colonel, informing him about the enemy army's locations and movement. When her uncle became ill, he arranged for her to marry Gregory John Babykin, who was an army captain. She later became an army nurse.

Anatole "Greg " was born in the American Hospital at Istanbul on November 28, 1922. His refugee parents were in Turkey working with the American Red Cross to get visas to enter the United States. The Babykins, including Greg's three-year-old sister Tatiana, entered the U.S. at Ellis Island on July 1, 1923, when Greg was nine months old. Legally, he was a natural born citizen of Turkey, but that technicality wouldn't surface until much later.

When the family arrived at the Port of New York, they were met by members of a church group that took them to Stamford, Connecticut, where Gregory John worked for the church and the

Yale Lock Company. While the family was in Connecticut, daughter Tatiana had an accident and died. Soon after, the family settled in Queens, New York City, and became part of a community of transplanted Russians that observed many of their old traditions, retained their native language and their reverence to the Eastern Orthodox Church. In 1927 Gregory and seven others started what later became the Lion Match Book Company in New York.

Young Greg went to religion classes after his regular school day and made his first communion and confirmation as he might have in the old country. Gregory John and Tatiana had two more children, Gregory V. and Julianna, after they made their home in New York.

Clearly, Greg's early life was tumultuous, but as the family settled into New York life he became imbued with the values his parents had fought for in the Russian Revolution and Civil War. He was patriotic, appreciative of what the U.S. offered his family and was happy to join the fight to keep the nation free.

In 1937, the Babykins moved to Astoria on Long Island and Greg enrolled in Bryant High School. There he distinguished himself as a football and track star, winning first place in the New York City 400 and earning an athletic scholarship to Duke University. He started college in September of 1941 and played on the freshman football team. Greg and his teammates had a game on December 6, 1941. The next day, the Japanese bombed Pearl Harbor; the day after that Greg and the entire football team signed up to go to war.

In 1942, while waiting to go into active service, Greg took a job at Macy's in New York. He married Edna Eggers on November 8, 1942; and in January 1943 he reported for active duty with the Army Air Corps. He took his basic training at Tulsa, Oklahoma, and reported as an aviation cadet for training as a pilot in Independence, Kansas. While in aviation training, he came down with the measles. Only a week after recovering from the illness, Greg had to demonstrate his ability to fly. Unbeknownst to him, the measles had caused him to lose his depth perception. He failed his flight test because he couldn't see well enough to land the plane. Consequently, he washed out of pilot's school and was assigned to gunnery training in Kingman, Arizona.

After finishing gunnery training, he was accepted to bombardier/navigation school in Deming, New Mexico. Next, in February of 1944, he reported to Hammer Field near Fresno, California, where Frank Jeter was assembling his B-24 bomber crew. Jeter selected Greg as his crew's bombardier and the die was cast for his entry into the Pacific War.

By this time, Greg and Edna had their first child, Gayle, and Edna went with Greg to March Field near Riverside, California, where the Jeter boys were assigned as of April 7 to an overseas training unit. Edna was able to stay at March Field during this time, as were other Jeter Crew wives (who have kept in touch with each other since). On June 22, the crew left for Seattle where they would ship off for Hawaii on the Fourth of July 1944. Greg would not see Edna and Gayle again until November 1945 when he was released from active duty at the end of the war.

Back home after the war, Greg's parents urged him to make immediate plans to go back to college. He re-enrolled at Duke University, and just two months after he returned to New York, he was in class picking up where he left off. Edna recalls a remarkably changed atmosphere in the university town of Durham, North Carolina, after the war. "Everyone was older and you could tell they were veterans. They wore their old leather jackets and khaki pants," she said with a laugh. "It was different too because many more of the students were married and had families, so the university had to provide more services, like married student housing."

University campuses were full after the war accommodating the veterans who were going to school on the GI Bill. Although Greg had gone to Duke before the war on an athletic scholarship, most of the Babykins' friends had not. "The best result of the war was the GI Bill (a 1944 law establishing financial benefits for World War II veterans returning home)," Edna said. "All these boys got to go to college. Before the war and in the Depression they never even thought about going to college. They couldn't afford it."

The Babykins found their home in a big, two-story house that had been split up into apartments for student families. The children were safe playing in the back yard away from traffic, and the families helped each other out. The rent was cheap at $25 per month, and the women had use of a big bathtub to wash the family's clothes. Money was tight in Greg's college days, and Edna recalls shopping strategically to stretch each dollar. "If I knew that carrots were 2 cents cheaper at one store, I'd walk there rather than buy the more expensive ones at a nearby store," she said. Greg planted a garden—as he had done in the Pacific where soil was fertile—so the family had a good supply of vegetables. The landlady also had a beautiful garden and on Sundays they enjoyed taking a walk to see its latest blooms.

"We also had the college football and basketball games for entertainment," Edna recalls. "Greg was in charge of hiring students as ushers for the football stadium. Married men got the first choice (of assignment). After the games, our friends came back to our apartment for a spaghetti dinner. The weekend was fun; Monday it was back to the books and work."

Edna has fond memories of the times in Durham, but she also remembers the difficulties. "It was a struggle for the boys. Some of them couldn't concentrate on their classes and some didn't make it. Some of them had nervous breakdowns. It was an emotional change for them to have to study. They needed time to get used to being civilians." Greg graduated from Duke with a degree in electro-mechanical engineering in December of 1949 and went to work for a time at the phone company as a linesman in Middletown, NY.

On June 25, 1950, the Korean War began and Greg, a member of the New York National Guard, was called back to active duty immediately. Edna and Gayle were able to stay with Greg in Texas while he took his training. Despite the seemingly difficult circumstances, the Babykins' experience in Texas turned out to be a good one. Edna recalls with fondness her days in New Braunfels, a community half way between San Antonio and San Marcos.

While Greg was on duty on his first day in Texas, Edna went out looking for a place for the family to live. She walked down the main street to a real estate office. The agent was out to lunch so she walked back down the street. As she passed a drug store, a man came out to greet her and asked her if she was in trouble. "It was hot, so he said 'why don't you come in and have a cold drink?'" she recalled. "So my daughter and I went in and sat at the counter of the soda fountain." She began to visit with the others at the counter, and she told them her husband was stationed at the air base and she was looking for a place to rent. "One man piped up and asked another man 'isn't your house in escrow and vacant?' And the other guy said, 'well, I guess I could rent it, but you'll have to clean it up.' I said okay!"

Then she asked if anyone could recommend a babysitter to take care of Gayle while she worked. Someone there knew someone who could babysit and asked Edna where she worked. "I told them I was looking for a job, and someone else said 'well, there's a job open at the courthouse'. . . So within an hour, I had a house, a job and a babysitter!"

Being called back up for war might have seemed like a disaster for a man with a spanking new university degree. But for Greg it turned out to be a second chance to pursue his dream to become a pilot.

"Because he had been in the Army Air Corps during the war, he was able to get into flight school again," Edna related. Greg reported to San Marcos Air Force Base in Texas for his flight training and this time he earned his pilot wings. As a pilot and experienced combatant, Greg again entered the service, this time to support the war against communism in Asia and Eastern Europe. The enemy was North Korean communists who were backed by the Soviet Union, the next generation of Bolsheviks who had forced his parents out of their homeland. [7]

---

7 The Korean Conflict, which lasted from 1950 until 1953, was a battle to keep communist powers from taking over Asia. At the Potsdam Conference at the end of World War II, the Allies split Korea at the 38th parallel with Russia to control North Korea and the United States to support South Korea.

After Korea, Greg didn't even get home before he got a job at General Electric. He was passing a GE plant in Schenectady, New York, still in uniform, when he stopped impulsively and applied for a job. He worked 13 years for GE in Johnson City, New York.

In 1966, he went to work for the engineering department at NASA (National Aeronautics and Space Administration) and worked as a quality control engineer primarily on the Apollo Space Program and on the design of space flight simulators. He was with the team working on the Black Hawk and the Seahawk helicopters. "He sat in front of the instrument panels, and as a pilot he knew where all the controls should be. So he could tell them (the designers) what changes to make," Edna related. He also worked on the early versions of airborne warning and control systems (AWACS), which are aircraft equipped with special radar and communication systems designed for surveillance. He also consulted on the development of the "heads-up" helmet, which allowed pilots to see critical controls without looking away from the sky.

When Greg went to work for NASA, he had to become an American citizen before the government would give him the security clearance needed for the work. He went through the process and was granted his citizenship on June 27, 1966.

Greg worked part-time as a back-up pilot for several commuter airlines while working for NASA. He retired from the Army reserves as a major in 1972, and in 1982 he retired from NASA and the airlines. Shortly after retirement, he was able to enjoy his Russian heritage with a trip to his homeland where he and Edna connected with his relatives who had stayed in Moscow.

Greg was active with the Sister City organization in nearby Binghamton, which exchanged visitors with Borovichi, Novgorod Oblast, Russia. When tour groups came from Russia, Greg escorted them around the city showing them the American way

---

7 CONTINUED The U.S. entered the conflict with the backing of the United Nations when the North Korean communist government sent troops across the border into South Korea. The war was never declared and never officially ended. Fighting stopped when an armistice was negotiated in 1953 and a demilitarized zone established at the North-South line.

of life, including schools and public infrastructure. As an engineer who spoke Russian, he could explain the inner-workings of the city so the visitors who didn't speak English could understand. "He'd get them settled in their hotels; he'd take them shopping, show them how to pick out a shirt, show them the schools; they were very interested in seeing the water and sewer plants, just how we did things in the U.S.," Edna explained.

Greg and Edna, married 67 years, had daughter Gayle and two sons, Gregory, Jr., and Gary; and four granddaughters, Anastasia, Ashley, Adrian and Avery. Greg was interviewed for the "Jeeter Bug" documentary and attended its premiere in 2004, but he passed away in 2009. Edna remains in Apalachin, New York, where she and Greg lived for 50 years.

CHAPTER 14: HERB HARTER, CO-PILOT

Jeter Crew co-pilot Herb Harter already had lots of experience flying an airplane when he joined the Army Air Corps at 19. Growing up in Amarillo, Texas, Herb learned to fly while he was in high school. He and about 20 friends pooled resources to buy a single-engine, two-seater 1930s-built Aeronca.

They took lessons from local flight instructors at the Amarillo Airport, and Herb soloed in his junior year. He described the 65 horsepower aircraft: "There wasn't much there, it was very small and not too strong. It was just nuts and bolts and stuck together." He remembered that it cost $1.20 in gas and oil to fly the plane for one hour.

Herb also flew as a student in the Civilian Pilot Training program begun by the government in 1939. A student at Amarillo College in the fall of 1941, Herb was one of the thousands of American boys who participated in the program meant to "fill the sky with pilots" in anticipation of the U.S. entry into World War II.

He recently recalled the first day of basic flight training at Thunderbird II Air Force Base in Arizona where his pre-war experience was unusual among the pilots in training. His instructor, an old rough spray pilot, confronted Herb about his maneuvers during a solo flight. "What the hell are you doing up there?" the instructor demanded. Feeling his oats, Herb replied: "Aerobatics, sir!" "Show me!" the instructor demanded.

So Herb climbed into the front seat and the instructor got into the rear and they took off. Herb did a few rolls and a loop and then another maneuver called an English Bunt: From level flight you put the nose straight down and keep going until you are going the opposite direction. You are upside down hanging from your seat belt with Gs forcing blood to your head. Herb looked in his mirror and noticed the instructor was hanging limply in his harness — out cold!

Herb landed the plane as the instructor was coming to. When the plane rolled to a stop the instructor climbed down and said,

"Okay. Just keep your head out of your ass."

His early experience as a pilot no doubt emboldened Herb to face the challenges of sharing the helm of a B-24 in the dicey days over the Pacific Ocean. The aircraft was much bigger, some would say lumbering, and there were the Japanese to contend with.

Other members of the crew found Herb to be strong, competent and tranquil most of the time. "(Herb is) a good pilot and has just as much guts as the old man (pilot Frank Jeter), and I think is inclined to be just a bit calmer," Dale Henderson wrote about Herb in the first months he knew him.

Today, more than 65 years later, Herb says he was seldom afraid while the Jeter Crew was in the air. "I never had a fear. It didn't bother me that much. I wasn't frightened. I knew I had to do my job. I never had the thought that I wouldn't come back."

But he admitted that being 18 or 19 had a lot to do with his bravado. He also acknowledged some scary in-flight incidents. He remembered training at Kahuku on Oahu before the crew went into combat. "We lost guys in training. Some people had trouble and went down." He recalled one return flight when the Jeter Crew ran into clouds that stretched to within a few hundred feet above the ocean.

"We were flying so low we were almost touching the huge waves below, and we didn't know if we'd be able to find our way back to base. Ray Fritter had everybody in the back praying we'd make it. Luckily, we were in touch with Island Command and they helped us break through the clouds.

"Over-ocean flying was different. When we were training in the states we had landmarks like railroads and rivers to help us find our way," he continued. "But over the ocean we didn't have anything to go by and it could be frightening. We relied on John (Weller), and he always got us through. Sometimes he questioned himself because the islands out there were so small you could miss them if you were a little off course."

Two untoward incidents marring the Jeter Crew's missions stand out in Herb's mind. The first was when Sam Tillery and Doyle Ebel had to straddle the open bomb bay doors to dislodge and jettison a live bomb that didn't drop over the target as expected. "That was very scary," Herb recalled. (See Chapter 9 for more detail.)

The second was when the plane lost an engine when taking off from Guam and barely had the power to get aloft. It was the co-pilot's job to salvo the bombs in such a circumstance. "I had a lever in front on the left side of my seat. But I had to wait until we cleared the hospital that was just off the end of the runway," he remembered. Luckily, the plane picked up power minus the bombs and the crew flew back around and landed, aborting the mission without tragedy. (See more about this in Chapter 8.)

For Herb and Frank, however, landing safely was not the end of this nightmare. "The Allied High Command said we had to find those bombs and recover them," he recalled. "We searched and searched for them. We used machetes to cut through the thick foliage of the jungle. We had their location pinned down to an area about the size of a city block, but we never did find them."

Herb Harter was born December 3, 1923, in Edinburg, Texas. His father, Herbert C. Harter, a Kansas native, was an oil and natural gas investor; his mother, Edna Newman Harter, was born in Iowa. His parents divorced when he was five, and Herb stayed with his mother who managed motels and hotels in Amarillo. He graduated from Amarillo High School in June 1941 before enrolling in Amarillo College, a two-year community school. He enlisted in the Army Air Corps as an aviation cadet one week after Pearl Harbor, but he wasn't called for active duty until March of 1943.

Herb was assigned initially to the Air Corps basic cadet training at Santa Ana, California. He and an Amarillo friend, Bob Izzard, traveled to Santa Ana together on the train. Bob's father was Wes Izzard, a famous Texas Panhandle journalist and broadcaster.[8]

---

8   Because Bob's father was well-connected, Herb always wondered if Wes had arranged for the train compartment he and Bob shared on the trip to California. Bob Izzard became a fighter pilot in Europe and was shot down over German-occupied France. He was rescued by the French underground who helped him get back to England after 100 days in enemy territory. After the war, Bob followed in his father's footsteps as a broadcast journalist and wrote several books on the history of the Texas Panhandle.

Next, Herb reported for primary flight training at Thunderbird II Air Base in Phoenix, Arizona.

He finished in August of 1943 and went directly to Pecos, Texas, for basic and twin engine training. While there, he developed jaundice and missed a month of training. He graduated on March 12, 1944, receiving his wings and the rank of 2nd lieutenant. The same month, he arrived at Hammer Field in Fresno, California, where he was assigned to the Frank Jeter Crew.

After the war ended, Herb went back to Texas and served in the Air Corps reserves. He employed his expert skills as a flyer to teach civilians in Dumas and Panhandle, Texas, for about a year and then opened his own life insurance agency in Dumas. While working in Dumas, he met his future wife, Roberta Medlen, a home economics teacher. They were married in 1949 and settled in Dumas where they lived for the next 65 years. They have two children, David, born in 1952, and Mary Ellen, born in 1956. David is a communication consultant; Mary Ellen is an artist.

Herb started out small, but through the years his agency grew to represent a number of insurance companies. He made a success of it and was honored by his peers in the insurance professionals association as a member of the Million Dollar Round Table for 31 years. He was active in the Dumas Lions Club and the Chamber of Commerce. For the Lions, he produced a promotional video to orient new members to the club and worked on many community projects throughout the decades. For the chamber, he also worked on various projects, including raising funds to rejuvenate the town's holiday decorations in 1965. Continuing his close association with aviation, Herb served on the Moore County Airport Board for 15 years.

Dale Henderson visited Herb in Dumas and witnessed firsthand his status in the community. On a visit to a local department store, several "little old ladies" stopped Herb to ask him about a town issue. "He is a pillar of the town, twice receiving the Citizen of the Year award... He is known and respected by just about everyone in the community." Herb retired in 2002 and in 2012, he and Roberta moved to Dallas to be near their son.

The Jeter Crew members' commitment to preserve their wartime friendships throughout their lives is a source of amazement for Herb. Even today, the remaining crewmates keep in touch despite the distance that separates them. "I talk to John and Jo Weller all the time," Herb related from his new home in Dallas. "Through all these years, we've continued our friendship." He lamented the passing of Greg Babykin in 2009. "We stayed close all those years. He was kind of grumpy and gruff sometimes but he had a big heart. He was a great guy. I hated to see him go. Frank (Jeter) and I were close friends until he died (in 1989). Dale Henderson was a good friend."

In his diary of the crew's early days together, Dale observed that Herb was "the best liked officer on the crew and a swell guy to have at a drinking party. He stays sober and pays most of the bills." Sixty-plus years later, Herb recalled his place in the crew's social order: "I was the one who always had money in my pocket. If the other guys ran short, I would loan them money until pay day. They usually paid me back when they got their pay checks."

Chapter 15: Dale Henderson, radio operator

The night before the Jeter Crew shipped out of California for Oahu and the Hades known as the Pacific War, radio operator Dale Henderson sat down and started a diary. The first — and only entry for 57 years — is dated June 27, 1944. In it the budding man from Iowa and California revealed his innermost thoughts, and he admitted to himself that he feared going to war. "I have just turned 21, and I guess the next year will be the toughest I have yet had to face and maybe the roughest I will ever have.

"Being a radio operator on a B-24 bomber I guess in the next few months I am going to see plenty of action. Knowing I will see planes with my buddies go down in flames and thinking that it could have been me, I sometimes wonder how I and my crew will stand up under the pressure. That is why I am writing this diary so that I can look back and see my reactions to my partaking in World War II."

Henderson pondered his decision to stay on active flying status even though the doctors had diagnosed an arthritic arm that could have grounded him. "I don't want to die. The reason I'm on the crew is that I don't think I will die, and I want to be able to say to myself that I helped in this thing. I don't think I want to be a hero. I just want to go over and do my job and then get the heck back and get my education. I know I'm going to be one scared GI when that first burst of flak comes up or when that first fighter comes in with guns blaring."

A thinker by nature, Henderson often mused about the irony of life. A few weeks earlier, he had been floating in a boat at Wilshire Park in Los Angeles when he and his date heard about the Normandy invasion on the radio. "I knew it would not be long before I would be in combat. It was a funny feeling knowing how peaceful and serene it was there and at that very moment thousands of miles away many fellows my age were being killed. I had an inkling, but was soon to learn that those who never experience war can never really know what it is all about."

Later, when the crew found themselves unpredictably on embattled Iwo Jima, Henderson was the one who absorbed the irony of finding salvation on a pockmarked runway they'd been bombing mercilessly a few weeks before. He was the one who recorded each of their missions with pertinent emotional detail and often put them in perspective. (See Appendix for Dale's description of missions.)

After the war, Dale wrote personal accounts of some of the especially scary missions. For instance, he told the story of the "high speed stall" with a certain poignancy. It was on a ferrying mission from Guam to Okinawa in June of 1945. Pilot Frank Jeter pulled the plane out of a dive at the last moment and acted somewhat nonchalantly about it. Dale wrote in a report years later that he was worried to death they wouldn't survive that flight.

Dale had a generally positive attitude. In the films taken by his fellow crew members he always appeared perky and happy and gave a cheerful (and cute) face to the camera. In his diary and other writings, he always gave credit and praise to his fellow crewmen. He considered himself lucky to be part of the Jeter Crew — and to survive the war. But one could argue that at times he didn't seem lucky at all.

On July 31, 1945, 12 days before the end of the hostilities in the Pacific, Dale was seriously injured in a runway accident involving two crashes and the death of 23 men. He was burned over most of his body and required hospitalization and plastic surgery that delayed his release from the service until August of 1946. (See Chapter 9 for more detail.)

You could say Dale was lucky in spite of this horrible incident. He lived to have a good life after the war. In his memoir, Dale tells the rest of his story: "I had married Bernice Messer on November 23, 1945. We had met while I was on rest at Hickam Field, Hawaii, in March. When I was discharged Bernice was pregnant with our first child so I enrolled at Morehead Teachers College at Morehead, Kentucky, so we could be near her parents' home when the child was born." He went on to have four more children, all girls, and to have a successful and happy 38-year career as a high school history teacher and administrator in Portland, Oregon, schools. "I loved every minute of my teaching career."

During the war, Dale was the one who best understood the significance of the relationships among the crew members. After enduring a tumultuous childhood, he had found the brothers he was missing as an only child from a broken home. Having formed bonds with his crewmates, he recognized how important it was to keep everyone together for life.

Dale A. Henderson was born Dale A. Sell in Chester, Nebraska, on June 25, 1923. His father, David A. Sell, and mother, Lucindia Mae Voight, divorced when he was two. The next year, his mother married Jack Henderson and the family moved to Lake Manawa, near to Council Bluffs, Iowa. His stepfather moved the family again to Long Beach, California, in 1929. They made the trip in a 1925 Model T Ford and traveled on the partially built Route 66. The trip took two months and the Ford suffered many flat tires on gravel roads. They arrived in Long Beach on New Year's Eve. Dale was in first grade.

Dale laments: "Jack Henderson was an alcoholic, and the marriage was in a constant state of flux. Between 1930 and 1937, I spent a year in a sanitarium, a year with a relative in Council Bluffs, and two years in a boarding home. I was in the seventh grade when I was finally able to live a rather normal life with my mother."

Dale graduated from San Fernando High School in Los Angeles area on his birthday, June 25, 1942. He lettered three years in gymnastics and was senior class president. He was awarded a scholarship to Pomona College upon graduation.

He was inducted into the service on January 16, 1943, and got his basic training at Hammer Field in Fresno, California. In March, he enrolled in the meteorological cadet program at Pomona College. "I washed out May 18 and shipped back up to (Fresno). There they told me I had a choice of gunnery, gunnery or gunnery. So I took gunnery plus radio." Dale graduated from gunnery school in Yuma, Arizona, on February 16, 1944. After he "laid around" at Fresno from February 29 until April 5, he shipped out to March Field where he would meet the rest of the Jeter Crew.

Washing out of the meteorology program was a blessing in disguise for Dale. When he went back to visit his Pomona College colleagues during his furlough between Yuma and his return to Fresno, he learned the program had been discontinued. Most of his fellow cadets had been sent into the infantry and were part of the division that was caught up in the Battle of the Bulge in Belgium in December of 1944. Looks like he dodged that bullet.

Dale would also consider himself fortunate to get on Frank Jeter's crew after being pulled off two previous crew assignments that were never meant to be. "The night before leaving (Hammer Field) for survival school I was taken off the crew and told to report to the medical board (for his arthritic arm). . . I was assigned to another crew and was shipped to March Field. Just as I was alighting from the bus my name was called, and I was taken off the crew and made a casual. Two days later a pilot came looking for a radio operator and chose me. I took a check ride the next day and thereby joined the crew of Lt. Frank Jeter."

In 1979, 34 years after the Jeter Crew officially disbanded, Dale Henderson got wind of a reunion of the 11th Bombardment Group in Denver, Colorado. Dale contacted everyone—at that time everyone was still alive—and practically demanded they all meet up there. He succeeded in getting all but three crewmates to attend. The only three missing were engineer Bob Larson, nose gunner Vic Crowell, and ball turret gunner Sam Tillery. In future years all mates would assemble at subsequent reunions and family events and keep in touch by telephone. "Dale was responsible for getting us all together after the war. He said that we were his family because he never had a family of his own," navigator John Weller recalled. Doyle Ebel added: "I was an only child and he was an only child and we found each other. He (Dale) was looking for a family and we were it."

By the time of the Denver reunion, Dale and Bernice had separated and she was not planning to attend. But when the rest of the crew found out that she wasn't coming, they put pressure on Dale to get her to interrupt her bus trip from Portland to Kentucky to meet them in Colorado. They got a message to her in Phoenix and she caught a bus to Denver and arrived the next day. The Jeter Crew ultimately got Bernice to the party and then all was right with the world for the nostalgic ensemble. Dale notes in his account of the reunion: "The women got together at poolside. Bernice had arrived and there was much to talk about."

Dale was also responsible for recovering the Jeter Crew films taken during the war. At the reunion, Dale learned that pilot Frank Jeter had the films stored somewhere at his house in Dallas. Dale urged Frank to dig them up and turn them over so he could see what was there and make them available to the crewmates. Dale got the rolls from Frank, had them converted to VHS (video tapes), and gave everyone a copy. Ultimately, these films would be the basis for the "Jeeter Bug" PBS 2004 documentary that told the story of the crew's emergency landing on Iwo Jima.

In 2001, Dale was instrumental in compiling lifetime bios of each of the Jeter Crew members. For comparison, he revisited his 1944 diary entry that included short bios of the individuals as he then knew them. "Now 57 years later I look back at these words with a smile. I am certainly glad I took the time to write them. Words are hard to come by to adequately express my feelings and thoughts of these men. During the years that I taught I often told my students that I was a very lucky man, almost blessed, for I had the opportunity to be with a group of men in such close circumstances. . .The bond that developed was one built on respect and trust and developed into a deep love. . .I would not trade this relationship with these men for anything in this world. It is a bond that can only be forged in war or at a time of severe hardship and stress."

Dale recalls a time long after the war when he suffered a heart attack and his "brothers" rallied around. "I was in intensive care, and of course, they only allow you to communicate with family when you're in intensive care. The day after I had the attack the nurse came to Wanda (Dale's second wife) and asked: 'Does he have a brother in Chicago?' and about ten minutes later she came back and asked: 'Does he have a brother in Honolulu?' and Wanda said, 'yes, yes, oh yes.'

"Well, all the crew called that day and I had to tell the nurse that I was on a flying crew during World War II and these are my brothers, we are family. We all love each other, that's it, we're that close."

Doyle Ebel laughs when he relates the same story: "Dick (David) would call and say he was Dale's brother from Chicago; I would call and say I was his brother in Texas. And the nurse asked Dale: 'how many brothers do you have anyway?' "

Dale's lessons on World War II and his personal experiences were not lost on his students. In 1998, one of Dale's former students contacted him to belatedly express her sense of wonder and respect for World War II veterans. After seeing the movie "Saving Private Ryan," Jill Dunn, married and the mother of a young son, wrote to Dale: "You taught me a lot about our nation's government and history, but by sharing your own war experiences, you also showed me that the everyday men who put down their tools and picked up weapons of war because it was the right thing to do, and it was necessary, were heroes and all Americans owe them deep debts of gratitude.

"How can I ever adequately thank those who sacrificed so much — not just their lives, but also their innocence, their jobs, their families and so much more?" she wrote.

After retiring in 1987, Dale bought a second home in Toutle, Washington, in the shadow of Mt. St. Helens, and the brothers gathered there from time to time to renew their bonds. "We thought he was crazy to buy property facing an active volcano," Doyle said. "But it was really beautiful up there."

Following an 11th Bombardment Group reunion in Nashville in 1990, Dale published a collection of interviews with Air Corps veterans who survived the Pearl Harbor attack on December 7, 1941. The book is titled: "Lest We Forget. The *Gray* Grey Geese Remember." Dale writes in the introduction: "Many of the men had just come off maneuvers. They were young men, most in their late teens or early twenties. It was a lazy Sunday morning, Dec. 7, 1941, until 0755 when the attack began."

In his final diary entry in 2001, Dale reports: "Bernice and I had five daughters. The oldest passed away, but all five are college graduates. There are 12 grandchildren. Bernice died (recently) of kidney failure and I will remarry on December 5, 2001, in Honolulu, Hawaii. Wanda L. Parten is the bride-to-be."

Dale and Wanda were married at the Hale Koa military-only hotel on Waikiki Beach, Honolulu. His brothers were there. Dale was in a wheel chair and very ill with bone cancer on his wedding day. He surprised Doyle by asking him on the spur of the moment to be his best man. "He just said: 'here's the ring,'" Doyle said.

Sadly, Dale died two months later on February 6, 2002, in Portland. He will never know that his efforts to keep the crew together and to preserve the films of their war experience would result in the "Jeeter Bug" documentary, which was produced in 2004. But the film and his honest and insightful writings will keep his memory alive.

CHAPTER 16: DOYLE EBEL, TAIL GUNNER

Doyle Ebel showed up for war with the intention of making the best of it. He'd withstood hardship growing up in Houston, Texas, during the Great Depression, and he accepted the challenge of war in much the same way.

Log-keeper and unofficial crew scribe Dale Henderson writes of his initial impression of 20-year-old Doyle: "He is damned glad to be in the Air Corps and fighting the war in a half-way decent manner. He's a darn, swell boy, plenty steady . . . Ebel is mighty grown up for his age, maybe it's the responsibility of marriage. . . Another hard fellow to figure out and yet the more I think about it there isn't anything *to* figure out."

Like pilot Frank Jeter, tail gunner Doyle Ebel enjoyed the lighter side of war. Dead serious on a mission, Doyle knew how to exploit his leisure time in between nightmarish bombing forays. Doyle and pal Dick David, the radar operator, were the "best scroungers" in the U. S. Army Air Corps, according to their fellow crew members. Ever resourceful, they scrounged mattresses for their night-time comfort, they scrounged for food, which was often scarce, and they horse traded for hard liquor and beer of all kinds.

A great storyteller, Doyle loves to recount his escapades in scrounging for the Jeter Crew. He set up a dark room in a trench where he developed film and printed photos for fellow airmen. He traded with combat photographers, exchanging beer for supplies. He used his cunning ways to acquire and squirrel away liquor for the much-anticipated end of tour crew party. He and Dick found breakfast for the Jeter Crew when they were stranded on Iwo Jima with a crippled B-24.

Stationed as tail gunner at the far back of the plane, Doyle liked his vantage point when the bombs were dropped. "I could always hang out the back of the airplane and I could look out to see where the bombs hit," he recalls. Doyle also kept a sharp eye out as he moved around the cabin and frequently spotted land before anyone else.

Doyle recalls a time when radio man Dale Henderson came to the tail to see him. "He looked around, and said, 'You're crazy sitting back here. You're a fool. I wouldn't sit back here for nothing, hanging out here like this.' "

When at his tail gunner position, Doyle fought the below zero temperature by wearing a heated suit and boots. "It was so cold back there your breath would freeze," he recalled. At times, when intensely involved in a fire fight, he would forget the cold and the adrenaline kept him warm. On one occasion, his left foot froze under him as he knelt to work the tail guns. To this day, he still suffers pain in that frostbitten foot.

Doyle Victor Ebel was born March 17, 1924, in Houston, Texas. His parents, Emily and Walter, both natives of Brookshire, Texas, had moved to Houston during the building boom of the 1920s. Walter was a house builder and found plenty of work until the Great Depression hit the entire country in the mid-1930s. Doyle got a paper route when he was 12 and kept the job until his senior year of high school. He had taken auto mechanics courses at school and when he was 17 the local Ford dealership offered him a full-time job as a mechanic. Doyle took night classes to complete high school and graduated in January 1943.

Just two months later, on the day after his 19th birthday, March 18, 1943, Doyle was drafted into military service. What happened in the next year or so must have made his head spin. First, he went to Miami Beach, Florida, for basic training. While in Florida he came down with the measles. He finished basic training and reported to radio school at Scott Field, Illinois, in June of 1943. On the Fourth of July, he became ill with pneumonia and had to be hospitalized for 42 days.

When released from the hospital he was given a 14-day leave to convalesce. Doyle took advantage of this break to go home to Texas and marry his childhood sweetheart, Pattye Louise Hambrick. Next, he returned to Scott Field to enroll in fire control school. Ironically in view of his later career as a fireman and petro-chemical fire expert in Houston, the class was abruptly cancelled. In January of 1944 he was assigned to gunnery school instead. After graduation, he had 10 days leave before reporting for duty. He zipped home to see Pattye, and then reported to Hammer Field near Fresno, California, where he was assigned to Frank Jeter's air crew destined for the war in the Pacific.

While Doyle was flying over the Pacific, his father joined the home front war industry, working as a pattern-maker in a shipyard in Houston; Pattye worked in a weapons factory that made 8-inch cannons.

When the war ended, Doyle returned home to Houston and took back his job as a mechanic at Johnston Ford. Not surprisingly, he was soon bored by the job. How could he settle back into a mundane occupation after fighting his damnedest to endure the rigors and danger of war? He represented the classic case of "How you gonna keep 'em down on the farm after they've been to Paree (Paris)?"

Looking for excitement, he found it with the Houston Fire Department. He joined the department in 1948 and worked his way up the ranks over the years. In 1963, he was promoted to district chief and was assigned to the area that included the Houston Harbor. The district also included the large number of petro-chemical companies concentrated along the 50-mile shipping lane from Galveston to Houston's port.

In this capacity, Doyle worked with the petro-chemical companies, many of which had their own fire department as part of an unusual cooperative public-private firefighting agency. "The city of Houston couldn't offer the type of protection that was needed, so each company had to have its own fire brigade," Doyle explained.

In his role as harbor district chief, Doyle developed a vast knowledge of how to fight petro-chemical fires and soon became a sought-after seminar instructor in major cities across the nation. He also became an expert on ship fires and wrote the Houston Fire Department's procedural manual for shipboard firefighting. In the course of his career, Doyle was offered administrative positions but he declined, wanting to remain in the field. He preferred to be on the scene fighting fires and directing crews rather than working in an office.

Pattye and Doyle have three children: Melody, Roger and Judy. Roger is a retired fireman and Judy married James Rick Booth, a captain in the Houston Fire Department. Melody married Clenton Wilson, an engineer for the Harris County (Texas) Toll Road. The senior Ebels have six grandchildren and seven great grandchildren.

In 1969, Doyle graduated from South Texas Junior College (now part of the University of Houston System) with his proud family in attendance, including his first grandson.

A Christian before going to war, Doyle's faith only deepened during his time in combat. The Jeter Crew comprised four Catholics, four Baptists, one Mormon and Doyle, a Lutheran. One of the Catholics, Ray Fritter, was very devout and was destined to become a priest when he returned to California. Doyle found inspiration in Ray and the air crew's chaplain, an Irish Catholic priest. "I came from a Lutheran background, and we were always taught that Catholics weren't the best of people. I had to change my mind when I met Catholics for the first time (in the service).

"The chaplain was a great man. He would always be there to pray for our safe return from a mission. And then he was on the air strip again when we came back to see if we needed any (spiritual) help. Of course, he gave the last rites to the deceased," Doyle recalled. Ray served at the altar with the priest in makeshift chapels that were set up crudely when the squadron moved to a new base; and Doyle tagged along with him to the Catholic Mass.

Doyle remains religious today and recently shared his harrowing war-time experience with his pastor at the Tree of Life Lutheran Church in Texas. After viewing the "Jeeter Bug" video, Pastor Chris Lake gave a sermon about how the light of Jesus had shined on the Jeter Crew the night of the emergency landing. "I was reminded . . . that there are no atheists in fox holes. That rings true, but it rings just a bit truer when you hear it from one who has been in a fox hole, or in the back of a B-24 that has lost (two of its engines) and needed to land on Iwo Jima."

CHAPTER 17: DICK DAVID, RADAR OPERATOR

By the time Chicagoan Dick David joined the Jeter Crew in 1944 he'd already been through hellish jungle fighting and deprivation on Guadalcanal and had handled radio on B-17 crews in missions to bomb Rabaul, Japan's most fortified position in the Pacific. He'd been to India to learn radar techniques from the British and had flown 13 missions with A-20 crews bombing Japanese convoys traveling the embattled Burma Road in the China-Burma-India area. He'd participated in 13th Air Force softening up operations for the invasion of Tarawa and Makin in the Gilbert Islands, and he'd flown sea search missions in B-18s while he recovered from jungle rot and malaria at Hickham Field on Oahu, Hawaii.

On Guadalcanal in September of 1942 at the height of the six-month battle, Dick used his skills in guerrilla warfare learned in training in Hawaii to stay alive in desperate conditions. He carried a machete as well as a revolver to defend himself in the jungle. "You couldn't use a gun because when you fired, the blast would identify your position to the Japanese soldiers," he recalled. With the 27th Infantry of the 25th Division, Dick's unit was stranded on Guadalcanal without adequate supplies when Japanese battleships drove away the unloaded U.S. Navy supply ships. "The ships left because they had no protection (from Navy battleships whose crews were not prepared to fight at night)," he explained.

Dick described his Guadalcanal experience by saying: "I was 19, and I didn't think I would ever be 20... We had nothing down there, we were short of all the things we needed. We had a C-ration once a day, and sometimes we would have a K-ration once a day... The guys used to say: 'No mama, no papa, no Uncle Sam."

On Guadalcanal, the army infantry and the marines mingled in their encampments. "The marines were all kids like us," Dick recalled. "We were near the Tenaru River and the Japanese would come down from Rabaul and shell us almost every night." On one particular night, Dick and two other soldiers were sleeping in their fox hole and were blown out of the hole by a shell from a Japanese cruiser that anchored nearby. Suffering from concussion and a debilitating knee injury from the blast, Dick was laid up for a time and was confined to the communications tower they called "The Pagoda". Fortuitously, he was invited by Laverne "Blondie" Saunders, the commander of the 11th Bombardment Group, to fly a mission to Rabaul as radio operator.

"When we got back he asked me, 'Do you want to stay in the infantry, or would you like to fly with us.' I said, 'well, that's a no-brainer," he recalls with a laugh. Still walking with a cane due to his knee injury, Dick flew 20 missions to Rabaul and Bougainville from Guadalcanal's Henderson Field with Saunders's group. The group started out with 27 B-17 aircraft and at the end of three months, there were only seven or eight left. Dick served as radio operator and as waist gunner: "I was so darn lucky that I never got shot up."

In December of 1942, Dick was assigned to radar training conducted by the British in India. Most of the training was in flight, and Dick participated in 13 A-20 night-time bombing missions over Burma with the 10th Air Force in early 1943. "We'd be over the target and the target was the road (Burma Road) and we'd pick up a Japanese truck convoy. Once we had it lined up, we'd turn on our landing lights; we'd have it in our sights so we could see very plainly and then we would strafe the blazes out of them."

In April of 1943, Dick was assigned to the 7th Air Force and went back to Hickham Field for more radar and bombing training. In July he went to Canton Island with a joint Army-Navy communications unit to help prepare for the invasion of Tarawa and Makin. During this time, he participated in photo reconnaissance missions to both islands. In November of 1943, he was sent back to Hickham because he was sick with malaria and jungle rot. While recovering, he went on sea search missions, working as radar man.

In March of 1944, Dick was assigned to the 26th Squadron of the 11th Bombardment Group on Kwajalein and worked for nine months as an on-call radar operator. Meanwhile, the Jeter Crew was serving with the 392nd Squadron of the 30th Bombardment Group on Saipan. In January of 1945, Dick was assigned to join them as their 11th member and radar operator. His first mission with the Jeter Crew was on Jan. 3, 1945, to Iwo Jima; it was the crew's eighth mission.

Once with the Jeter Crew, Dick made good use of his experience both as a radar operator and as a deprived infantryman. He joined up with tail gunner Doyle Ebel as the "two best scroungers" in the Air Force. Doyle (or "Ebie" as Dick calls him) likes to tell the story of how Dick was savvy with military forms and was able to dummy up a truck driver's license when the Jeter Crew was on rest on Oahu and needed transportation to get to their favorite swimming hole.

Richard A. David was born April 23, 1923, in Chicago, Illinois, to Marcel and Catherine David. His father was an agent for the Internal Revenue Service. He ran track and was active on the student council at Charles Schurz High School in the heart of Chicago before graduating in the spring of 1941. While in high school he was a member of the Civil Military Training Corps and was trained both as an infantryman and as a corpsman. He got an early start on a life-long career in banking while still in school by working for the First National Bank of Chicago.

In January of 1942, Dick was called to active duty and sent to Camp Roberts, California, to join the 72nd Division of the U.S. Army. There he was trained as a radio operator in an intelligence and reconnaissance unit. In May of 1942 he boarded a ship bound for Hawaii where he joined the 27th Infantry of the 25th Division. He was trained in guerrilla warfare and sent to Guadalcanal where he was initially assigned to work behind the lines in communications.

After the war, Dick joined the reserves as a master sergeant. He returned home to Chicago in December of 1945 and helped to form the 437th Troop Carrier Wing at O'Hare Field in March 1946. He was on flying status as a radar operator and head of the radio communications unit and was given a direct commission into the Air Force in 1947.

Six months after returning home, Dick married Jacqueline Norris in the summer of 1946. They had a daughter, Michele, in 1947. He returned to his job at the bank and took classes at night at Loyola University. In 1951, he was called back to active service with the outbreak of the Korean Conflict. His troop carrier unit was sent to Korea, but Dick was sent to Carswell Air Force Base in Fort Worth, Texas, to join the Strategic Air Command, 7th Air Division, 406th Squadron. He joined a B-36 crew as electronic counter-measures officer and flew surveillance missions over Russia.

In 1952, he left the SAC and went to Air Defense Command as a radar operator stationed at Larson AFB at Moses Lake, Washington. During this time, Dick graduated from the Industrial War College of the armed forces. He separated back to the active reserves at the end of 1952, and in July of 1966, he retired as a major.

In 1953 he enrolled at Bishop Shields International School at Loyola and received a bachelor's degree in international studies in 1958. That same year, he helped organize a mosquito abatement district covering 300 square miles of Northern Cook County. In 1966, he went to work for the Central National Bank of Chicago to establish its International Banking Department. In 1971 he was instrumental in establishing Banco di Roma (Italian Bank) Chicago as a state bank and also setting up branches in the Midwest. He retired in 1986 as Senior Vice President and Operating Manager.

In retirement, Dick has continued to be on the mosquito abatement district board and has served as secretary/treasurer and trustee. Sadly in 2008, his beloved wife of 62 years, Jacqueline, passed away.

CHAPTER 18: VICTOR CROWELL, NOSE GUNNER

Victor Crowell was born in 1925 in Big Lake, Texas, a tiny community known best for its proximity to oil fields discovered not too long before his birth. The Crowell family later settled in nearby Lamesa where his father, Louie, ran his own construction business and his mother, Henrietta, was a homemaker.

When Vic was 16, the Japanese bombed Pearl Harbor, pulling the U.S. into the war and changing life drastically for everyone in Texas — and everywhere else — overnight. In 1941, Vic was a star athlete at Lamesa High School where he had distinguished himself in football and track. His attention was quickly diverted by the prospect of learning to fly to help win the global war for the United States.

The bushy-haired, eager teenager quit his milk delivery route in 1942 and got a job working part-time at the glider school at the Lamesa airfield, which later became an Army Air Corps training base. The experience intensified his desire to become a pilot.

At 17, Vic convinced his mother to sign for him to join the U.S. Army Air Cadet program. Before graduating from high school in June of 1943, not only had he enlisted, he had also gotten married. On April 26 of that year, Vic and his longtime girlfriend, Betty Jo Sumpter, said their wedding vows.

Betty recently recalled life in Lamesa before the war: "We went to church every Sunday. Everybody went. Church, football, school and the movies — that was our social life." On the day Pearl Harbor was attacked, Betty was at home eating popcorn when the news came over the radio. Later in the day, everyone in Lamesa attended church service to pray for the boys who had lost their lives, and for their loved ones.

"Everybody got a phone call to come to the (First Baptist) church, but since it was on a Sunday, we all would have been in church that night anyway… I was grown up and married before I learned that not everybody went to church every Sunday," Betty said with a laugh.

Come October, Vic said good-bye to Betty and his family and was enrolled in aviation cadet training at Wichita Falls, Texas. But that assignment was only a stint, ending when his entire class was washed out, and he was sent to gunnery school in Harlingen at the southern tip of Texas. Betty recalled recently how disappointed Vic was that he couldn't be at the helm of a warplane. "He loved flying. He was always reading books about planes and flying." But, she said, he bided his time and picked up on his boyhood dream to become a pilot after he returned home at war's end.

Following his gunnery school graduation in February of 1944, Vic was assigned to Hammer Field in Fresno, California, where he became the nose gunner on Frank Jeter's B-24 crew. Next, it was Kahuku airfield on Oahu where the crew got their advanced bomber training. His place on the crew was one of the most dangerous, sitting in the front of the plane protected only by Plexiglas. "He said he was always shaking up there, and he didn't know whether he was shaking so much because he was cold or because he was scared," Betty recalled.

In his diary, radioman Dale Henderson recorded his first impression of Vic: "Cpl. Victor Crowell, nose gunner. I get a laugh just thinking about him. Not that he is one of those everlasting comics. It's just that he is the baby of the crew. Eighteen, yet he is married and to a very sweet girl. Crowell is a swell kid with plenty of what it takes. The only trouble is that he is still a kid, but combat will change that. He is the assistant engineer."

As assistant engineer, Vic worked with engineer Bob Larson to conduct preflight checks and to keep the B-24's systems functioning properly in the air. He was called upon to dig in with Larson when the crew was bringing the plane back to life after the emergency landing on Iwo Jima in March 1945. Pilot Frank Jeter put Bob Larson and Vic in charge of the repair while the others took orders to pitch in where needed. Vic climbed up above the engine to help remove and replace the shot-up engine.

Victor Crowell was discharged from the Army Air Corps in November of 1945 and went home to Lamesa to work with his dad building houses. He took lessons at the local airport and fulfilled his dream of becoming a pilot. Betty says Vic spent many hours in the air with his trainer and flew to places like Colorado and New Mexico. He flew solo and acquired all the essential flying skills. Betty never flew with Vic in a private plane, but the Crowells enjoyed many outings to air shows and other aviation-related events.

A year later, on November 1, 1946, Betty Crowell gave birth to their daughter Vicki. Their son Daniel was born on June 19, 1953. "He was a good father and a good provider," Betty said recently.

In 1962, Vic landed a subcontract to help build the administration building of the George Bush International Airport in Houston. That job led to another, and Vic decided to move the family to Houston where he worked for major construction companies and contracted for his own jobs for the next 23 years. While they lived in Houston, Betty worked for the school district where she served as a secretary whose duties included qualifying underprivileged children, mostly offspring of Mexican immigrants, for special programs.

"Some people (in the community) thought it was terrible that they didn't speak English. They said, 'they need to learn the language or they should go back to Mexico.' I just thought, 'we are all immigrants, coming from another country at some time, and we needed help back then too.' People would say things like: 'They are taking the jobs from our citizens.'

"They worked and they worked cheap, as laborers, not within a union," she continued. She said they were doing necessary jobs, many of which American laborers wouldn't do. Betty said she knew that they didn't stand a chance for a good life in Mexico, if they went back. "They (the children) were legal and they had *nothing*," Betty recounted. "I worked to help those children. I was happy to do it. I just thought if we don't educate these children they are going to grow up and have to be on welfare.

"Victor worried about me going out into the (poor) neighborhoods to interview the families (to qualify them for free lunch). Often, only the children could speak English and one of them interpreted for the parents. Some of them got to be my friends. I taught them how to fill out the forms needed to get help. I wasn't afraid," Betty recalled.

In his leisure time after the war, Vic often took his family on camping trips and forays into remote natural spots where they would dig for rock treasure. He had the tools to cut and polish the family's finds of crystal, opal, turquoise, topaz, quartz, and other minerals and turn them into bolo ties and jewelry. [9] Vic and Betty were members of the local mineral and gem club: "We were rock hounds," she said. "The whole family enjoyed it and it was something we could do together." They also hunted for arrowheads and amassed an impressive collection that they donated to the Texas History section of the Jasper, Texas, museum.

Vic was an outdoorsman and liked to take Betty and the kids out where they could sleep under the stars with a lean-to tied to two trees. "We used to look up at the stars and find the constellations," Betty remembered. They also used to hunt and fish. "We had a quiet, happy life."

"We went to every air show we could," recalled Betty. "There was one show we went to every year at Midland-Odessa put on by the Confederate Air Force (now Commemorative Air Force)." [10] There they would witness a reenactment of the bombing of Pearl Harbor. "Old planes would go up over the airfield and they would drop artificial bombs. There would be World War II planes out there. There were B-24s on display there, and the Thunderbirds would fly over. We didn't miss anything that came near to Plainview."

The couple also volunteered to help at their church, Trinity Fellowship Church in Plainview, working on the food for the poor

9   A bolo tie (sometimes bola tie or shoestring necktie) is a type of necktie consisting of a piece of cord or braided leather with decorative metal tips—aglets (aiguillettes)—secured with an ornamental clasp or slide. Source: Wikipedia

10 The Commemorative Air Force, originally known as the Confederate Air Force, is a nonprofit educational organization dedicated to preserving, in flyable condition, a complete collection of aircraft flown by all the military in World War II. Source: http://commemorativeairforce.org/

program and fundraisers. Vic was on the usher committee. The Crowells' son Daniel attended Wayland Baptist University and graduated in 1993. He suffered liver failure at age 41, and died while waiting for a liver transplant.

Vic rarely spoke of his experience on the Jeter Crew. But when he and Betty got together with the other crew members he reveled and relished the good moments. "It's just amazing how they kept meeting after the war," she said. "They talked and enjoyed each other so much. Those men were talking all day. The women went shopping and when we came back they were *still* talking and laughing."

Betty remembers wartime in Lamesa vividly. At 17, she worked at the ration board and experienced the shortages that people endured. "We had to give up our mattresses (for the steel innersprings) and people had to have stamps for everything—food stamps, stamps for gasoline, stamps for tires. People drove around with slick tires (that had lost their tread). Sometimes, I think about all the times I drove around in cars with bald tires!" She also recalls the busloads of boys leaving for war. "The war brought people so close together. I remember the time fondly. We never thought about locking our doors. It was a different world."

CHAPTER 19: RAY FRITTER, WAIST GUNNER AND SPIRITUAL GUIDE

In 1931, when Ray Fritter was eight years old, his father died suddenly of a heart attack. Vernon C. Fritter had been fighting a forest fire near Chico Meadows in Northern California and after the excitement was over, he dropped dead while pulling a fire hose. Ray's father, only 49 at the time, was part of the Fritter family whose ancestors settled the community of nearby Durham in the 19th Century. Ray had been born on the Fritter ranch in 1923, and his roots there were deep. His father, who had worked as a blacksmith in Stirling City, was buried in the Chico Cemetery close by. The funeral was conducted by a minister from the First Christian Church, and the Knights of Pythias, an anti-Catholic lodge to which Vernon belonged, did the honors at the graveside. (The Vatican prohibited Catholics from belonging to this lodge in 1883.)

Ray's mother, Amelia Willmann Fritter, originally from the San Francisco Bay Area, almost immediately moved her four children to San Jose, California, where she had family. She enrolled Ray in St. Leo's Catholic Elementary School where he had some difficulty adjusting. His attitude at first was: "Those nuns will never convert me!"

At age 10, Ray was baptized a Catholic. He continued at St. Leo's and graduated from Bellarmine Catholic boys high school in 1941. Almost 20 years after being baptized he joined the Dominican Order. He was ordained a Catholic priest in 1956 and served a lifetime as a generous man who counseled and ministered to prisoners at the Oregon State Penitentiary, helped bring new life to marriages as a parish priest and served as treasurer to the Dominicans' province administration.

In between his baptism at age 10 and his adult commitment as a Catholic priest came his experience on the Jeter Crew. This World War II duty as a waist gunner required him to fire shots at the enemy and to help to accomplish bombing missions against strategic Pacific islands. How he reconciled the violence of war with his faith we may never know, but he didn't ever seem to stray from the Jeter Crew's commitment to win the war. What we do know is that Ray Fritter served as an inspiration to each member of the crew as they forged through enemy skies to make their missions count.

Dale Henderson wrote in his diary of his first impression of Ray: "Cpl. Raymond Fritter, he is Sammy's (Tillery) assistant and the exact opposite (referring to Sam's unrelenting interest in meeting girls). He is a Catholic and a very religious boy. Sometimes I actually believe that he thinks there is no wrong in the world. He is a swell fellow, and I think a heck of a lot of this guy, yet I think just as highly of the rest. Ray is also from San Jose (like John Weller) and is 21. I will see him in actual combat more than any other for he and I are the waist gunners.

"It's really hard to put into words," Doyle Ebel said recently when discussing his relationship with Ray Fritter. "We were very close. We all had tremendous respect for him. We followed him to Catholic services (at the chapel on the various islands where they were stationed). Ray served at the altar with the Catholic priest. We helped to build the chapel on Okinawa because there wasn't one. We all worked there."

Ironically, Doyle didn't think too much of Catholics before he met Ray Fritter and other Catholic members of the crew (John, Greg and Dick). "I was raised a Lutheran. I went to Lutheran school. We were part of the Missouri Senate of Lutherans. We were the first group who broke away from the Catholics (in America). I was taught that Catholics weren't the best of people. But when I got to know these guys I thought: 'Hey, these guys ain't bad. I changed my opinion. There's nothing wrong with them. They are just like me.' "

Aside from his devotion to his faith, Ray Fritter had another side: he enjoyed life and was resourceful. While on rest on Oahu, he took surfing lessons and later he developed into an accomplished downhill skier. He liked to make puns and entertain friends and colleagues with singing and music. While stuck on Iwo Jima the crew relied on Ray to be the Boy Scout who built a fire to make coffee on that first morning after the emergency landing.

Ray Fritter was discharged from the U.S. Army Air Corps in November of 1945. He went back to San Jose and enrolled in the winter semester at Santa Clara University, a Catholic institution. The next year, he transferred to San Jose State University where he graduated in 1949. Coming from a family of meager means, Ray was always finding jobs to supplement the family's income. While in college, Ray worked part-time at a haberdashery renting tuxedos. Later, he and a friend, Quiten Smith, set up S&F Tuxedo Shop, which rented formal wear for college dances and weddings. He soon grew tired of the business, sold his interest and decided his destiny was to become a priest. In August of 1950, he entered the novitiate in Kentfield, California, and took the name Christopher.

Fr. Paul Scanlon, OP, a Dominican priest who knew Fr. Christopher (Ray) Fritter, OP, wrote his fellow priest's obituary in 1985 after Fr. Fritter succumbed to liver cancer: "Novitiate life was not easy for him, and he showed the quality of perseverance under difficulty that was to see him through challenging assignments later on. Studies did not come easy through his years of formation, but he found enjoyment in being photographer for *The Dominican,* a province vocational magazine of that period.

"Chris (as they called him in the order) was notorious for his inevitable puns and his great social charm. He loved singing old Broadway musical numbers, fishing, camping, skiing and being part of the innocent joy of jovial gatherings of song and humor," Fr. Scanlon wrote.

After his ordination in 1956, Fr. Fritter took a series of assignments as parish priest, serving in Seattle, Washington, and Benicia, Antioch and San Francisco, all in California. In 1961, he was assigned as chaplain at the Oregon State Penitentiary in Salem, Oregon. This was a tough assignment: Chris was taking over for pioneering prison chaplain Fr. William Joseph McClory, OP, who was the first full-time chaplain hired by any of the Oregon state penitentiaries. Fr. McClory had been highly respected and loved. He had succeeded in convincing the prison officials to build a chapel separate from the main prison complex. Fr. Scanlon wrote of Fr. Chris's work with the inmates: "… he found this no easy task. Typically, he reached out for help and guidance from others and made of his six years there a time of dedication and service."

It was during this time that Dale Henderson saw a lot of Chris (Ray) as the priest traveled from the prison to the ski slopes. "Since he loved to ski and our home was on the route between Salem and Mount Hood, he was a frequent guest for dinner during the winter months. Our daughters always looked forward to the visits of 'Fr. Fritter.' He served as chaplain for six years. In 1967 the provincial (head of the Dominicans in the Western region) asked him to serve as treasurer of the province, another difficult position which he fulfilled with skill and dedication," Dale wrote. Fr. Scanlon described his time as treasurer: "Chris was humorously known for his financial pie charts to explain province expenditures, and he became adept at trading automobiles."

A quote in a 1972 Utah newspaper article caught a glimpse of Fr. Fritter's style in handling his treasurer duties: "It's a minor miracle that Fr. (J. H.) Valine has survived in Milford and southern Utah for 25 years, considering the rigors of his varied efforts," Fr. Fritter told the newspaper. The article continued: "Fr. Fritter left Milford with a better understanding of the problems Fr. Valine faces in operating the church farm lands (in Milford Valley)." Fr. Fritter was in charge of financial matters for the Dominicans' 25 Catholic missions in the territory west of Denver, from the northern U.S. border with Canada to the southern border with Mexico.

Fr. Fritter returned to parish work in 1973, and he was assigned to St. Dominic's Catholic Church in Benicia, California. He first served as assistant pastor for five years and then he became the pastor and superior in 1978. At St. Dominic's he was a founding member of the local chapter of the Knights of Columbus and served as the charter chaplain. "Sociable by nature, he found the Marriage Encounter movement much to his liking and devoted much time to that," wrote Fr. Scanlon. Marriage Encounter helped Catholic married couples renew and deepen their commitment to each other through weekend retreats.

While Chris was parish priest at Benicia in 1979, he received a call from radio operator Dale Henderson insisting that he attend the reunion of the 11th Bombardment Group in Denver, Colorado. Having taken a vow of poverty, Chris (Ray) didn't have means of his own to make the trip. John Weller explained: "He had to ask the Dominicans for the money to attend the reunion." Fortunately, Chris (Ray) was able to get transportation to Denver, and he was set to share a room with Dale who had planned to attend the get-together on his own.

At the last minute, Dale's wife, Bernice, was coaxed to Denver by the crew, and she too was to share a room with Dale, creating a situation that could have been embarrassing for everyone. John Weller loves to tell the story: "Ray (Chris) said: 'Don't worry about me. You sleep on your side of the room and I'll sleep on mine, and I don't care what happens over there."

Ray and his fellow B-24 flight crew members made the most of time shared during that first reunion in Denver. They reminisced about the good episodes of their unique war story and refreshed their friendships. As a special addition to the experience, Fr. Fritter (Ray) arranged to say Mass for the Jeter Crew at St. Dominic's Catholic Church in Denver, one of the Dominican Order's parishes. The reunion—together with the spiritual remembrances during the special Mass celebrated by Ray Fritter, now Father Christopher—gave the women a chance to get to know each other and their husbands better, cementing their connections with the Jeter Crew family.

Back in Benicia, Fr. Fritter served four more years as a parish priest. He found the time to trace the roots of the Western Province of the Dominicans and tracked down the location and photographs of the Order's first house in Monterey, California. He also worked with his father's cousin, Joy Fritter, and her family to trace the Fritter family's roots, going back to their 19th century life in Ohio. One of Chris's favorite projects was the renovation and improvement of the province cemetery, which was close to St. Dominic's in Benicia.

In 1983, at age 60, Chris and a close friend, Fr. Joe Beno, a parish priest from Salem, Oregon, whom he had met while at the prison, took off for a sabbatical pilgrimage to the Holy Land. Fr. Scanlon wrote of the priests' travels: "It was a glorious trip for both of them, and on his return, Chris stopped off to spend a semester with the Dominicans in Washington, D.C. It was in the following spring that the doctors discovered he was seriously ill with cancer of the liver."

Chris returned to California to be with his fellow priests at St. Dominic's in San Francisco. He spent the last three weeks of his life at St. Anne's Home where he was cared for by the Little Sisters of the Poor. He received countless friends and former parishioners, Fr. Scanlon wrote, and he met them as best he could with courage and humor. John Weller visited Ray in the hospital before his passing and met some of Ray's fellow priests. "On one occasion, Chris mentioned to one of the fathers that he was free for the Lord. He died peacefully on the morning of May 18, 1985, and is buried in Benicia in the cemetery he worked so diligently to beautify," Fr. Scanlon wrote in Fr. Chris's obituary. John and Jo Weller attended the funeral mass and wrote the names of all of the Jeter Crew members in the remembrance book.

Chapter 20: Sam Tillery, ball turret gunner

F or Sam Tillery, World War II was just the beginning of a long
and illustrious military aviation career. The son of an Arkansas
sharecropper, Sam quit school after eighth grade and went to
work at a grocery store in Little Rock. By the time he was 17 he
was trained as a sheet metal worker and was employed in the
West Coast war-time shipyards in Richmond, California. By the
time he retired in 1977, he had flown many types of fixed wing aircraft and helicopters, had been in charge of airfields in Huntsville,
Alabama, and on Kwajalein Island, and had taught the famous
German-born rocket scientist Wernher von Braun to fly a C-47
troop transport craft.

As armorer on the Jeter Crew, Sam's job was to maintain and
repair the B-24's guns and to make sure the bombs had dropped
out properly over the target. While in combat, Sam was crammed
into the ball turret gunner position at the bottom of the plane. The
tallest of the crew members, Sam agreed to take this dangerous
spot because everyone was afraid of it. "I was afraid of it too," he
said in a 2004 interview.

When Sam's wife Barbara saw a B-24 up close for the first time
years later, she cried when she thought of Sam stuffed into the
ball turret. Remembering the story of a close call involving Sam,
she was horrified to envision him straddling the open bomb bay
while getting rid of armed bombs that failed to drop out during
a mission. "They had no parachutes and nothing below to keep
them from falling out," she said, referring to Sam and Doyle Ebel
who had to get the bombs out of the aircraft before they exploded
and blew up everyone. "It's a good thing Sam has such long legs,"
she said, "since he had to straddle the open doors. I felt the tears
just streaming down my face as I looked at the space in the B-24
and imagined what could have happened."

Barbara, who met Sam after the war, believes he was extremely
lucky to survive all the dangerous situations the Jeter Crew

confronted on their bombing missions. She also considers herself fortunate to have met Sam and shared a rich life with him during a postwar career that took them many places, including exotic and beautiful places in Asia and Europe.

Samuel E. Tillery II was born February 3, 1924, in Collegeville, Arkansas, just outside of Little Rock, the state's capital. He was the youngest of Samuel E. Tillery, Sr., and Carrie Beatrice Thompson's five children. The family was poor: Sam's father worked in a sawmill but became a sharecropper when the mill closed during the Great Depression. Sam left school at 13 to earn money for the family. He took sheet metal classes at night and left home at 17 to go to California looking for war production work. He was originally bent on going to Southern California to get on at the Lockheed aircraft factory, but he learned on the train that industrialist Henry Kaiser was paying more for metal work in his Richmond shipyards in Northern California.

Sam spent two years working in the Kaiser shipyards, and in June 1943 he was drafted into the Army. He asked for infantry but was assigned to the Army Air Corps and sent to Kearns, Utah, for basic training. Next he went to armory school at Lowery Field near Denver, Colorado, and then to gunnery school at the Army Air Field at Harlingen, Texas. Following his graduation from gunnery school, Sam was assigned to Hammer Field in Fresno, California, where B-24 air crews were being assembled. In March 1944, he was assigned to B-18, the crew being formed with Frank Jeter as pilot and leader.

Radio operator Dale Henderson wrote about his first impression of Sam in 1944: "Combat will really have to (come) before I will truly know about Sammy. He says he wants to get into the scrap very badly, but he confessed to me that he doesn't know how he will react. Confidentially, I'm not worried about a single fellow on the crew. Sammy will come through." Like the other crew members, Sam bonded quickly with his "brothers" in combat and took seriously his responsibilities to keep everyone as safe as possible.

Sam was released from the Army September 30, 1945, and returned home to Little Rock. There he sold meat for a while and then switched to selling cookies. Not thrilled about food sales, Sam decided to take advantage of the GI Bill and enrolled in aviation school and earned his pilot's license. In 1948, he joined the National Guard. With his experience in World War II combat, Sam was eligible to take a test to qualify as a commissioned officer. He passed the test and became a 2nd Lt. in the infantry, soon to be transferred to an artillery unit.

In February of 1950, Sam met Barbara Holland at a skating rink in Little Rock. He was immediately smitten. At the end of the evening, he asked if he could take her home. She declined because she was with her mother and aunt who had come to watch her skate, and because she lived 30 miles away in Sheridan. He got her phone number and said he would call her for a date.

Barbara recalled: "He called me and asked me out and I told him I couldn't go because I already had a date. So, he called me back again and I had to say no again. The third time he called I told him again that I was busy, so he said: 'Well I guess I won't see you again because I'm leaving for training in Oklahoma in a few days.' After he said that I said okay, and I broke the other date so I could go out with him.

"He asked me to marry him on our second date!" she recounted. "I told him 'you're crazy. You don't even know me!' He said he knew he wanted to marry me. Well, we continued to see each other and eventually I told him I'd marry him. He gave me a ring at Thanksgiving, and we got married when he was home for a few days at Christmas. We didn't have a big wedding. We just got married in the church there in Sheridan. We had to leave for Oklahoma right after the wedding."

While Sam and Barbara were dating, the Korean War broke out and Sam's National Guard unit was activated into the regular army. He was sent to Ft. Bragg, North Carolina, for field artillery training and, as a qualified pilot, he became an artillery spotter. He then went to Ft. Sill, Oklahoma, for more artillery training and next to Ft. Benning, Georgia, for CIA guerilla warfare training and jump school. "Sam really didn't enjoy jump school," Barbara recalled. She, on the other hand, wanted to sky dive. "I always wanted to see what it was like. But after I had children, I realized that I probably shouldn't take the risk."

Once he finished this training, Sam and Barbara went to Germany where he was assigned as a pilot and artillery officer for the 30th Field Artillery Battalion near the university town of Erlangen. At this time, the couple already had their son Sammy, who was five months old; and daughter Becky was born in nearby Nuremberg during Sam's tour of duty in Germany. Barbara described Erlangen as a beautiful, quiet city where the people were friendly and nice. The family lived in a 13-room German home, one that had been purchased by the U.S. government to house officers and their families. "The town was really nice. We enjoyed it there so much," Barbara said. Erlangen, near Nuremberg, is home of the University of Erlangen-Nuremberg, established in 1742. Erlangen was not an Allied target during the war, so the town was left largely unscathed by the hostilities.

Barbara said her Erlangen neighbors knocked on the door soon after the young family moved in. "They asked, 'Is your mother at home?' she chuckled. "I guess I seemed really young. They were these nice little old ladies. At least they seemed old to me at the time. They couldn't speak a word of English, and I couldn't speak a word of German. So whenever they came to visit, our maid would sit with us and she could tell us what the other person was saying."

Barbara said the young German housekeeper was a big help to her. "She loved Sammy so much. Once we traveled to Austria and she went with us to take care of the baby. She was so good with him." From their home in Erlangen, the Tillerys traveled to France, Italy, Switzerland and many other places in Europe.

While in Germany, Sam was promoted to captain and shortly after was sent to Ft. Rucker, Alabama, where he received advanced training in helicopters, multi-engine aircraft and became instrument-rated. Having completed this training, he was assigned to the faculty of the Army Aviation School at Ft Rucker.

Summoned to Tokyo in 1957, Sam was sent to Thailand, rather than Korea as he expected, and joined the 29th Engineers Battalion.

There he commanded a group of helicopter crews who supplied the surveyors as they worked to create a map of the Southeast Asian country. He started the job with seven crews flying H-13 Bell Helicopters and L-20 Beaver aircraft, but soon lost all but two of his pilots and all of his ground crews through rotation. According to Dale's Henderson's account, Sam "learned to be the best scrounger in the Army" and trained native Thais as mechanics "to the point they were rewinding generators." The mapping was finished by the end of 1957 and Sam returned to Tokyo where he served at the U.S. Embassy until 1960.

Sam's next move was to enroll in training that would prepare him for 13 months of duty in Vietnam. He rotated back to the states and took military intelligence training in Washington, D.C., and enrolled in jungle warfare school in Panama. In June 1962, he was promoted to major and assigned to the embassy in Saigon. But he soon became part of the Corps Tactical Operations under Col. Wilbur Wilson at Pleiku Air Force Base, Vietnam, and again was in charge of helicopters supplying the troops. When he returned home, Sam was assigned commander of the Redstone Army Airfield at Army Missile Command near Huntsville, Alabama.

Sam's assignment to Redstone was fortuitous because he had the opportunity to meet and get to know Wernher von Braun, who was the head of the U.S. Development Operations Division of the Army Ballistic Missile Agency and oversaw the Redstone Rocket project. One day Von Braun asked Sam if he would check him out as a C-47 pilot. "Sam gave him a book about flying the C-47 and von Braun memorized the whole thing," recalled Barbara. "Sam said, 'I don't need to teach you, you already know it all.'" Nonetheless, Sam took von Braun up, and after that encounter they became friends. Sam also checked him out on a Twin Beech (Beechcraft model 18 series aircraft). "From then on Mr. von Braun would always ask for Sam when he needed a pilot," Barbara said. "I met and talked to him at parties and I found him to be a really nice guy."

In the early 1960s, before Americans believed the space program could develop a ship that could land a man on the moon, von Braun was confident such an invention was not only possible, but probable. "Sam asked him, 'do you think we'll ever get a man on the moon?' and he said 'oh yes!'" she recounted.

Sam was promoted to Lt. Colonel and left Redstone in 1967 to start a new aviation school in Savannah, Georgia. He stayed there until November of the same year when he retired from the Army to take a private sector job with Sikorsky Helicopter. Sam quickly became unhappy in the Sikorsky position and took a civil service job as an Army test pilot. In 1969, he accepted a civilian job as a logistics and equipment specialist and moved the family to Hawaii. The job required a lot of traveling to Southeast Asian countries where he worked out of the U.S. embassies for weeks or months at a time.

Barbara was able to travel with Sam many times, and she got to experience various Asian cultures. "I loved going to different places and seeing how the people there live. I always liked to go to the marketplace and see their food and what the people were selling." Barbara recalled a trip to the Philippines where the local people had a fascination with her blonde hair. "They hadn't seen light hair before, so they wanted to touch mine. It didn't bother me but there was one time when Becky was with us and she was frightened by it. 'She said, 'mother we have to get out of here.'"

In 1974, Sam was offered a job on Kwajalein Island where he worked as contracting officer for aviation in the missile program. The family moved to the 6-square-mile island in the Marshalls, and Barbara got a job as a procurement analyst for the U.S. Army Corps of Engineers. The Tillerys found Kwajalein delightful. "There were no cars on the island, just bicycles. So we rode bicycles to work every day. I loved it there. There was a store there called Surfway, not Safeway, where they would get in new merchandise every week. So on Saturday we'd always go to see what they had. They always had bicycles, a solid bank of them parked in front."

Sam retired in 1977 from his civilian career and the family settled again in Honolulu, Hawaii—Waikiki, to be exact. They've stayed there ever since and love their Hawaiian lifestyle. Daughter Becky is in real estate in Honolulu, and she often rides her bicycle to work. "She loves it so much she has vowed to stay here forever. She won't even date anyone who doesn't plan to stay here," Barbara said with a hearty laugh.

When Dale Henderson and his wife Wanda were planning to marry in 2001, Dale asked Barbara to arrange the party. She set up the event at Fort DeRussy Beach Park in Waikiki and the Jeter Crew families came for the celebration. "It was great to see everyone. It was a beautiful wedding," she recalled.

At this writing, Sam is physically healthy but he suffers from short term memory loss. Barbara says he remembers some things about the distant past but never talks about the war. In the years when the couple traveled to 11th Bombardment Group reunions, Sam always enjoyed talking with the other crew members about their war experiences, keeping the bond between "brothers" intact. Barbara recalls when she first met the crew members: "They asked me if I was an airline stewardess because they said Sam always seemed to date stewardesses," she said with a giggle. She acknowledged that Sam attracted lots of women in his time. "Yeah, he did," she said.

Barbara concedes that she and Sam won't make it to any more reunions but she keeps in close touch with the other couples by phone. "It's just kind of amazing how well we've gotten along all these years," she said. "The wives became close, just like the guys did."

CHAPTER 21: BOB LARSON, FLIGHT ENGINEER

Born and raised on a Great Plains farm at the edge of the tragic Dust Bowl, Robert Lee Larson's life could be interpreted as an on-again, off-again love affair with the soil. He had farming in his soul, and no matter how many times he turned away from that life, he always came back. His mother's ancestors could be traced back 1,000 years as Norwegian farmers in the old country, and their tradition continued in the United States in eastern South Dakota on the Larson farm in Arlington.

Bob took up farming at age 14 in 1935 in the midst of a stubborn decade-long drought that devastated millions of acres of ill-fated grain crops that turned to dust. He gave it up in 1941 at the age of 20 and left South Dakota to pursue a more promising future as an aviation mechanic. "I told my parents, 'I just can't keep my plow in the ground,' " Larson told Jeter Crew mate Dale Henderson years later. He meant that statement literally and figuratively: he believed farming wasn't his calling, even though the troubled Upper Midwest region was finally showing signs of recovery, thanks to the long-awaited rain, as well as soil conservation help from the government.

But Bob would come back to the land over and over again in the ensuing 70 years. In between stints in the farming business, he helped fight World War II in the Pacific Theater, and even then found his hands were right at home in the dirt and grease.

Jeter Crew engineer Bob Larson was born October 1, 1921, in Arlington, South Dakota. His father was Hilder Luther Larson and his mother was Alma Mae Homerstand Larson, whose family in Norway was known for the centuries-old Homerstand farm. As a young child, Bob attended a one-room school house near Arlington. "All eight grades were in one big classroom," he recalled in an interview with Grace Provenzano for the "Jeeter Bug" documentary. "There were never more than 10 of us. I was in a class by myself for the entire eight years."

Bob played as a right guard on the Arlington High School football team. He played both offense and defense, and the team had a winning record. In Bob's senior year, the Arlington team won the South Dakota state football championship.

While he was in high school, Bob began to farm, and by the time he was 20 he was responsible for 480 acres of crops. He decided to quit at this stage and left for Wichita, Kansas, where he enrolled in aviation mechanics school. From there, he went on to San Diego, California, where he got a job with Consolidated Aircraft, the company that made many of the B-24 aircraft for the war. He advanced quickly in this environment because he was talented in all things mechanical. Shortly after his arrival, he was asked to help trouble-shoot problems with aircraft electronics, hydraulics and engine performance. He was recruited to work on a team testing the PBY-5A Catalina, the "American flying boat" used by all branches of the U.S. military during World War II and after.

In April of 1943, Bob was called up for the service and he joined the Army Air Corps. He took basic training at Fresno, California, and then went to Biloxi, Mississippi, where he learned more about aviation mechanics. He went to gunnery school in Laredo, Texas, and then joined the rest of the Jeter Crew at Hammer Field, back again in Fresno. Already familiar with the inner workings of the B-24, and other warplanes manufactured at Consolidated, Larson took the responsibility of engineer on the crew.

He seemed to have a healthy respect and a vigilant fear of the beloved Jeeter Bug. He knew its strengths *and* its weaknesses. The B-24 was fast, could carry quite a bit of weight and could go long distances to a target. But the plane definitely had its downside. "It was just a flying box car," Bob told Grace Provenzano in 2004. "I used to hate (getting the plane ready on the runway)," he recalled. "You'd go through each engine to make sure you had full power for takeoff. We'd have to rev it up to 30 degrees of mercury. The plane would just be sitting there trying to go and you've got the brakes on, you know, and it's shivering and shaking and just, oh, I hated that, especially when it was hot."

Larson's expertise and knowledge of the aircraft went a long way in saving the day when the Jeter Crew was stranded on Iwo Jima. Frank Jeter put Larson in charge of the repair the first day when the crew removed the prop in preparation for the new engine being brought in. Larson assisted the two mechanics who flew to the island battlefield the next day to help get the B-24 back in the air. "The fun time came when we tried to put that new engine in," Larson recalled. "You had these mounting bolts to put in. And you had these (battleships) lined up in a half moon behind the plane. So every minute or so, one of them would fire into the mountain or wherever they were going, and that plane would go up and down on its shocks three to four inches. So you had to time it just right," he said.

Bob's participation in the war, like many others, was a continuation of the struggles he had already experienced in life at home. Often, when the Jeter boys would get a day off while in training on Oahu, Bob would go along with Ray Fritter to work in the sugar mills for $7 a day. He was a poor boy who had learned the value of a dollar back home on the farm.

"I don't know if I changed that much," he said of his war experience. "The war probably gave me a better appreciation for life. I watched some of my buddies die."

Bob Larson was discharged from the Army in November of 1945. He took up farming again, this time in Forest Grove, Oregon. He married his first wife, Betty Herr, also in 1945. The following year, their son, Kim was born. A few years later, Bob and Betty divorced and he became discouraged by poor prices for his produce. He left Oregon, went back to San Diego and got a job working for H.G. Fenton Material Company as a truck driver and mechanic. Still restless, in 1962 he moved back to Oregon, this time to Springfield.

The Columbus Day Storm of 1962, the biggest wind and rain event in Oregon's history, had killed dozens of people and left many homeless. Storm damage was extensive and Bob realized there was an opportunity to relocate and start a roof repair business. While living in Springfield in 1963, he decided to become a member of the Church of Jesus Christ of Latter-day Saints

(Mormon). This association was one he relished and made a vital part of his life until the end of his days.

In the fall of 1965, Bob moved to Chico, California, where he opened a farm equipment business. He deepened his involvement with farming by purchasing four large combines and starting a custom harvest business. Before long, he traded his four combines for the largest harvester on the market. His business ballooned, and he and his crew traveled around Oregon and California 10 months a year helping farmers bring in their crops. He continued to operate the equipment business as well.

The story of how he met his second wife also has a farm theme. He was picking walnuts in an orchard near Chico when he encountered a woman who could harvest the nuts faster than he could. Her name was Larene Widdison. She was a Mormon from Idaho and a high school business education teacher in nearby Orland. The couple was married on February 10, 1967, in the Mormon Temple in Idaho Falls. They adopted their son Erik in 1968 and Ron in 1969. Then they had four sons of their own, Steven, David, Robert and John. Bob then had seven sons, including first born Kim. The family lived in Chico for 17 years.

Tragically, in 1980 Larene became ill with inoperable cancer. She died on October 31, 1980. Bob's youngest son, John, born on October 1, 1979, Bob birthday, was only about a year old when he lost his mother. Realizing he wasn't able to care for a baby on his own, Bob arranged for infant John to live with Larene's niece and her husband (the Gundersons) who raised him. In 1981, Bob moved with his six boys back to Oregon where he continued his harvesting and farm equipment business. He soon purchased Basin Construction Company in Klamath Falls and became a general contractor.

Bob remained in Klamath Falls for the rest of his life. He later started Larson Construction Company and specialized in steel buildings and metal roofing. He built many pole barns and replaced many roofs all over the Klamath Basin. Following his retirement, his sons took over the business, but closed it in 2011.

Bob took great interest in his church. He became an elder and spent countless hours researching family history. The goal of his research was to identify ancestors who could be baptized posthumously, and he traveled to the temple in Portland many times on their behalf.

Forever enamored with aircraft, Bob was interviewed by the Herald and News in Klamath Falls at an air show in 2007. "Bob Larson, 88 (he was really 86 at the time), crashed landed (the Jeter forced landing was not a crash) in a B-24 Liberator on Iwo Jima at 3 a.m. March 12, 1945, during fierce fighting," reporter Lee Beach wrote. "This aircraft didn't ditch very well," Bob told the reporter. "The marine sergeant told us to stay in the plane, which still had 1,000 gallons of fuel in it. He said if we got hit, we would never know it. We put a new engine in the plane, working on volcanic ash, not a blade of green anywhere, with just a few tools."

Beach continued: "Larson pointed out that the plane (on display) is 65 years old and the only one of its type still flying. Clint Smith, a contributor to the (Collings) foundation who was there for one of the flight experiences, took the ticket for his ride off his jacket and put it on Larson's neat grey suit. 'You can take the ride if you want to,' Smith offered. 'You probably just have to sign a release.' But Bob decided against it. "Larson was still considering it (the flight) as people started to climb aboard," Beach wrote.

Bob Larson died on October 31, 2011, ironically on Halloween, the same day Larene died in 1980.

Pacific over-ocean navigators:
Never let them see you sweat

By Capt. Bernard C. McPartland, Jr., *42nd Squadron navigator*

To say the least it was a bad situation. He was supposed to be a navigator, and yet he had no confidence in his ability to navigate. In navigation school he had done fairly well, but the missions had been too short and too mixed up. The navigation missions in phase training were worse. Bill couldn't think of a single flight that had given him the confidence he needed so badly at the present time.

Five minutes ago the major had come to his tent and told Bill that he was to navigate ship #939 to Johnston Island the next morning at 6 a.m. It was already 11 p.m. so Bill went to bed. A fine time it was to be making this trip. And what a trip! Between the Marshall Islands and Johnston Island there was nothing but 1,400 miles of water. And the trip was to be made during the day, so the only celestial body that he would be able to shoot would be the sun. A night trip would have been much easier. Why did the trip have to be made during the day? Well, the major must have a reason.

During the night Bill kept waking up. But he did get some sleep. When he was finally sleeping pretty well, someone shook him, "Hey, you going to navigate for us?"

"Ya" Bill groaned. They had breakfast, piled into a truck and went to the flight line. Bill decided that he liked the pilot who seemed to be one of those I-don't-give-a-damn guys.

Bill piled all of his navigation equipment into the nose of the plane where he was going to sit during the flight. This was a disadvantage because the nose of a B-24 is not very stable and it makes reading drift and taking celestial observations very difficult.

On takeoff Bill stood behind the pilot. As soon as they were in the air, Bill told the pilot to take a heading of 65 degrees. Bill then went into the nose of the plane. To make matters worse there was no way to check the compass. It might be right and it might be wrong, but chances are that it was wrong. Most of the compasses were, especially in the old war-weary ships like this one. The drift meter might be out of whack too, but chances are it was okay.

Bill decided that he would be able to trust the drift meter all right, because he had checked a lot of them, and he had never found any of them to be more than one degree off. And he knew that his octant was okay because he checked it a dozen times. He knew he could trust his drift meter and his octant, so there was a chance that they might make it to Johnston Island.

For the first couple of hours Bill took it pretty easy. He didn't want to wear himself out too much. He just read the drift, and told the pilot to change headings as the drift changed. The weather wasn't too bad, and things seemed to be going pretty well, except that Bill was worried sick. He wasn't too sure of anything. What the hell was he going to do if the time came when they were supposed to be over the island and no island was in sight?

After about two hours, Bill got up and shot the sun through the dome with his octant. He had to take a lot of shots and take an average because the plane pitched quite a bit. But he felt at least that he had a fairly accurate average. So he worked out the solution for the sun shot and plotted it on the chart. The shot showed him to be 20 miles right of course. Using this information he decided that his compass was 3 degrees off. It wasn't absolutely accurate but it was the best information he had. He decided to use it as best as he could, so he corrected the pilot's heading and went on hoping.

Bill sat back and tried to think the situation over. The whole trip ought to take about nine hours, he figured. After about seven hours of flying he ought to be able to get a noon-day fix. If the conditions were right this noon-day fix would tell him almost exactly where he was on the chart. Then he'd have two hours of dead reckoning navigation to Johnston Island. This might not be too bad.

But there were so many ifs. There was only a period of a half hour when he would be able to get the noon-day fix. If the sun was obscured during this period, it would be impossible to get the noon-day fix. Then he wouldn't know what the hell to do. Or maybe the air would be too rough to get a decent shot during the time for the noon-day fix. Bill continued to read drift and keep the plane on course as best he could. Occasionally he determined his ground speed by means of his drift meter and his stop watch, but he didn't have very much faith in this method.

About four hours out from the Marshall Islands they ran into a hell of a storm and the plane pitched and tossed like a row boat going over a dam. It rained to beat hell and the plane leaked. Both Bill and his charts were soaked. He couldn't do any more work on the chart, and it was the only chart that he had.

Never had Bill felt so defeated in all of his life. He found a dry piece of paper and proceeded to construct a new chart. He had always wondered why the hell they made him learn how to make charts. In contrast to the rest of the mess, it was one bright spot— he was sure that he knew how to construct the chart correctly. But it was pretty awkward with the plane still pitching, although it was no longer raining.

After about an hour they got out of the storm, and the air was smooth. Bill prayed that it would be like this when it came time for the noon-day fix. During the storm Bill was unable to read drift. He knew that he would be off course to some extent. Now that the air was smooth and the water was visible through the drift meter he was able to read drift again. At least he could maintain a pretty constant course.

He corrected the pilot to allow for the drift that he was reading at the present time. Then he sat back for a minute, gazing out over the water. The clouds below him were beautiful, but the thought of nothing but water for miles and miles depressed him greatly. He wondered why the rest of the crew was not worried, or apparently not worried.

Bill began to think about the noon-day fix. Only one more hour before he could take the fix. The interphone became clouded with conversation. "Wonder where the hell we are. Every time I look out it looks as though we are over the same spot. It's got me worried. Hey navigator, what's our ETA (estimated time of arrival)?"

"We'll be there about 3 o'clock Kwaj time."

"Okay, I guess I'll go back to sleep. What a hell of a long trip this is."

Then Bill heard the pilot: "Pilot to navigator." What did this guy want? He'd heard stories about some pilots.

"Go ahead pilot."

"Do ya want something to eat?"

"Ya."

"I'll send it up there with the engineer."

In a couple of minutes the engineer came up to the nose with some sandwiches and a can of fruit juice.

"How are we doing?" asked the engineer. For a second Bill didn't know what the hell to say. He was tempted to tell the engineer how he felt about the situation. He wanted to tell somebody! He disliked being alone in his apprehension. But he knew that he must display nothing but absolute confidence. If the crew lost confidence in the navigator, Bill would be in for all kinds of trouble.

After a second's pause, Bill answered the engineer, "We're right on course, and we're doing fine." The engineer left the nose compartment. Bill thought of the trouble he would have been in if he had taken the engineer into his confidence. In a couple of minutes the whole crew would have known about it. The pilot would be swearing, and the whole damn crew would be after Bill for the rest of the trip. Then the pilot would try to go into the island on the radio compass, refusing to fly the heading Bill gave him. If this happened they would probably fly all over the sky, and probably they would run out of gas. Ultimately they would make a water landing. Some of the crew might live through a water landing in the B-24, but the chances were not very good.

Bill continued to read his drift, correcting the pilot every so often. The air was getting bumpy. The time for the noon-day fix was approaching. Only 10 more minutes to go. For the noon-day fix he needed a number of good shots taken at intervals within a particular half hour. Bill bit into a sandwich. He was feeling pretty nervous. The time came and the sun was obscured. Bill stood by the dome with his octant in hand. A couple of minutes later the sun was visible. He hastened to get a shot. Even though the air was bumpy Bill continued to take shots. He continued to take shots until the sun went behind the clouds. He looked at his watch. He'd been shooting for three minutes. Obviously many of the shots were inaccurate, but he felt that he could get an average that wouldn't be too bad.

Bill looked into the clouds that were obscuring the sun. Ten minutes passed. He wondered, hoped, and prayed. The air was smooth now. Ten more minutes passed. The clouds seemed to part. The sun was visible. Bill looked through his octant. He knew now that he was getting good shots. The plane was very steady. For once he was lucky.

A couple of minutes later the sun was behind the clouds again. Bill started to work out solutions for the shots he had taken. After a couple of minutes he noticed that the sun was shining on his desk. He hastened to get another series of shots. The air was still smooth and he was able to get some pretty good shots. Anxious to see where the hell he was Bill worked out the solutions for the three sets of shots. Each set of shots would give him a line on his chart. The meeting of the lines would give Bill his position. If all three lines met at a point, Bill would be pretty sure of his position. This he did not expect, because he wasn't sure of the first set of shots.

When Bill finally got the lines on the chart, he found that the lines didn't even come close to meeting at a point; the lines formed a large triangle. Bill was frantic. Now he was lost for sure! But he knew he must not give up. He figured that one of the lines must be way off. He checked to see which line was most likely to be off. Then he checked over his solution. Finding a mistake, he worked the solution over and re-plotted the line.

Now it was a different story — the meeting of the three lines formed a very small triangle. Bill felt pretty good. At least he was doing his best. Now at least there was hope. Only two hours to go and he was pretty sure of his position. The fixes were by no means perfect, but he was pretty sure that it was accurate within 10 miles. But were they only two hours from Johnston Island? Bill checked the distance and figured the ground speed. From his figures he found that they were really two hours and 45 minutes from Johnston Island. He called the pilot, "Navigator to pilot."

"Go ahead navigator."

"Our ETA is 3:45 instead of 3:00."

"It's going to strain the hell out of our gas supply," the pilot said. "I figure we've got about three hours and 10 minutes of gas left. I hope we don't have to look for the damn island."

"We'll hit the island all right," said Bill with as much confidence as he could muster under the circumstances. Actually, he was scared stiff. It was such a small island, an island only 1 square mile was such a small spot on the ocean. Of course if the weather was good when they got there, they would be able to see the island from 20 miles away.

But Bill didn't expect the weather to be good when they got to the island. The weather had not been good along the trip. Why should it be good when they got to the island? He figured that if he did his best he could come within 10 miles of the island. If he came that close even in bad weather, they ought to be able to find the island by radio.

An hour after the noon-day fix they ran into soup. They were right in the middle of the clouds. They could not see above the plane below the plane nor could they see in any horizontal direction. For a solid hour and a half they flew through the soup with the plane bouncing up and down like a rubber ball. Drift reading was out of the question.

Bill figured that this hour and a half of not being able to read drift could throw them off course as much as 30 miles, but he decided to stay on course as best as he could. Although he knew that he was probably a good deal off course, he also knew that the closer they came to the island the better would be their chance of finding the damn thing.

About an hour out from Johnston Island there was a break in the weather. The air was smooth and the sun was shining. Bill got up and took a series of shots. The shots would give him only one line, but he'd know that he was somewhere on that line and that would be some help. The shots seemed to be pretty good.

When Bill plotted the line, it showed him to be 25 miles off course. Although Bill didn't know whether to believe it or not, it was all he had to go on. He gave the pilot the corresponding correction.

Ahead the clouds towered as high as 14,000 feet. The pilot decided to go below the clouds. Down 300 feet above the water Bill was able to read drift fairly well. He was by no means positive, but as far as he knew he was right on course. However he figured that his ETA could be as much as 15 minutes off. It looked as though the visibility were about three miles at the most.

At 3:45 the pilot called Bill on the interphone: "How close do you think we'll come? I don't know whether to trust this radio compass or not. This ship is old as hell, and the radio compass may not be worth a damn."

Bill answered: "We're right on course, but it may take us 10 more minutes to get there. Just stay on this heading." Though Bill wasn't convinced that they were on course himself, the pilot seemed satisfied.

The 10 minutes passed, and they could see nothing but water. The pilot began to talk, "The radio compass points to our rear, and we're damn near out of gas. "Pilot to crew, prepare for a water landing!"

Someone in the back started to speak, "I think I see a ship at four o'clock." Just then the island came into view almost directly ahead.

"Whew!"

DALE HENDERSON'S LOG OF JETER CREW MISSIONS:
NOVEMBER 1944 TO AUGUST 1945

1	Nov. 28, 1944	Iwo Jima	One flack hole, left vertical stabilizer. One fighter, Zeke, not aggressive. Flack from 90s north of south runway. Bombs away 15:35. Combat time 8 hrs. 10 min. Aircraft: *Salty Sal*
2	Dec. 5, 1944	Pagan	Milk run. Only three plane raid. No flack nor fighters. Bombs away 10:05. Combat time 2:50. Total combat time 11 hours.
3	Dec. 8, 1944	Iwo Jima	Big raid. 30th Group, P-38s, B-29s, and Naval shelling. Target closed, radar bombing, no flack nor fighters. Bombs away 13:25. CT 9:15. TCT 20:15.
4	Dec. 12, 1944	Iwo Jima	Hot one. About the only plane not hit by flack. Red Zeke, 12 o'clock, attacked before target. Silver Zeke at nine, not aggressive. Green Tojo out of sun, came within 150 yards of tail. Bombs away 13:30. CT 8:30. TCT 28:45.
5	Dec. 17, 1944	Iwo Jima	Cold one. Over target 1 hr., 12 min. Did radar bombing. One Zeke, 9 o'clock, not aggressive. Bombs away 13:05. CT 9:30. TCT 38:15. Aircraft: *Pacific Passion*
6	Dec. 24, 1944	Chi Chi Jima	Easy mission, long trip. Target less than 500 miles from Tokyo. Island socked in, radar bombing, 11 flack bursts. Bombs away 12:10. CT 9:50. TCT 48:05.
7	Dec. 30, 1944	Iwo Jima	Roughest flying weather encountered. Pea soup over target from 6,000 to 25,000 ft. Couldn't see wing tips, one mistake by a pilot and several planes would have gone down. Radar bombing. No flack, nor fighters. Bombs away 15:17. CT 8:30. TCT 56:35.

8	Jan. 3, 1945	Iwo Jima	Plenty of flack. #3 in C flight. Saw 28 bursts on port side. Around 150 bursts total. Babykin fouled up, our bombs in water two miles from island. Escorted Farmer back with #4 feathered. Bombs away 15:35. CT 8:55. TCT 65:30. Aircraft: *Sweet Routine*
9	Jan. 5, 1945	Iwo Jima	First night snooper. Dick really hot with radar. Babykin salvoed frag bombs, one exploded under us. Explosion spotlighted us, but searchlights didn't find us. One large fire started by earlier snooper. Bombs away 22:45. CT 8:55. TCT 74:25. Aircraft: *Jeeter Bug*
*	Jan. 9, 1945	Iwo Jima	Night snooper, turned back with two torching engines. Bombed Pagan. No credit. CT 5:40. TCT 80:05.
10	Jan. 14, 1945	Truk	Good show. We were one of a three plane decoy for P-38s to wipe out enemy fighters. They flew at 18,000 feet, we at 10,000, with cloud cover between us. Enemy thought we were sitting ducks. As they took off we radioed and the P-38s got most while still on the runway. Several did make it, but not for long. At 9 o'clock a Zeke made it to about 7,000 feet. A P-38 came down missed the climbing Zeke did a complete loop, hung on his props and blasted away. Zeke exploded. They got another, saw a parachute. Easy mission, no flack. We navigated P-38s back to Guam. One chick lost an engine and he tucked right under our wing. Great joint effort. No bombs. CT 7:45. TCT 87:50. Note: This mission was written up and called one of the longest over-water fighter missions of the war.
11	Jan. 17, 1945	Iwo Jima	Night snooper, easy mission, no flack nor fighters. Only thing wrong, it took all night. Take off at 21:30. 240 frag bombs away 01:45. CT 8.05. TCT 95:55.

*	Jan. 21, 1945	Iwo Jima	Night snooper, turned back. CT 6:35. TCT 102:30. No credit.
12	Jan. 25, 1945	Iwo Jima	Night snooper. Another easy one. Island open, clear as a bell. One burst of flack right under our tail. Take off 17:10. Bombs away 21:00. CT 7:45. TCT 110:15.
13	Jan. 27, 1945	Iwo Jima	Roughest yet, day mission, plenty of accurate flack. Hit lead plane – Bromer-90 right through the cockpit. Co-pilot and navigator severely wounded, also Bromer's right arm. After recovery brought plane back with one arm. Socked in around island, like a hole in a doughnut, Iwo clear as a bell. Small ship by island. Into the clouds after bombs away, Bromer out of control, almost hit us. We were #1, C flight, he was #3, A flight. We got one flack hole in top turret, missed Larson by two inches. Bombs hit target, some hit ship. We brought Bromer home, helped guide to landing. Take off 11:10. Bombs away 15:35. CT 8:20. TCT 118:35.
14	Feb. 1, 1945	Iwo Jima	Night snooper. Target clear, seven searchlights on us. Ray and Dale throwing out radar window like mad, Frank kept calling for more. Bucked headwind to target, made it home in 3:07. Take off 15:55. Bombs away 20:53. Landed 24:00. CT 8:05. TCT 126:40.
15	Feb. 5, 1945	Iwo Jima	Night snooper. Target socked in, yet five flack bursts. No damage. Up all night. Take off 21:15. Bombs away 01:30. Landed 05:10. CT 7:55. TCT 134:35.
16	Feb. 9, 1945	Iwo Jima	Night snooper. Good bombing, four searchlights but cloud shielded us. Had two run away props on take off, lost #3 on final approach. Take off 19:00. Bombs away 23:35. Landing 02:50. CT 7:50. TCT 142.25.

17	Feb. 15, 1945	Iwo Jima	Day mission, first in long time. Bombed by radar but broke clear just as bombs away. Target wide open, no flack. Estase spotting bombs jumped by three fighters. Good bombing. Weather out of Saipan 0'-0'. A real sweat job coming home, had to hit the deck. Take off 10:30. Bombs away 14:35. CT 8:35. TCT 151:00.
18	Feb. 17, 1944	Iwo Jima	The Big One. First pre-invasion raid went in 500-1000 ft. Right over Suribachi, strafed all the way in. Laid 250 lb. radio fused frag bombs over trenches on beach. Great bombing. Battleships Texas and New Mexico shelling all the time. Not much flack, also for 38th, but 27th caught Hell. 43 planes on mission. Saipan socked in on return, no problem landing. Take off 08:35. Bombs away 13:35. CT 9:15. TCT 160:15. Note: This is the mission that earned the Jeter Crew the Distinguished Flying Cross.
			Note: On March 1, 1945, crew and our plane, the Jeeter Bug, were assigned to the 26th Bomb Squadron, 11th Bomb Group, 7th Air Force and moved from Saipan to Guam. Until March 1, the Jeter Crew took off for their missions from Saipan.
19	Feb. 17, 1944	Iwo Jima	Invasion Day. Take off 02:35, bucked headwinds all the way. Arrived Monomi Rock 07:30, Navy would not let us bomb. Landed 11:40. CT 9:15. TCT 169:20 Note: On March 1, 1945, crew and our plane, the "Jeeter Bug" were assigned to the 26th Bomb Squadron, 11th Bomb Group, 7th Air Force and moved from Saipan to Guam.
20	March 3, 1945	Chi Chi Jima	Long mission. First one out of Guam. Target socked in up to 19,000 ft. After bombs away we went down to photograph Yome Jima, 25 miles north of Chi Chi, but broke over Ha Ha Jima. Gave it up. Take off 10:35. Bombs 16:30. Landed 21:35. CT 11 hrs. TCT 180:20.

*	March 11, 1945	Truk	Day mission. Turned back, #1 feathered. CT 1:35. TCT 181:55. No credit.
21	March 12, 1945	Chi Chi Jima	Night snooper. Take off 21:30, just as bombs away at 02:50 flack hit #2, #3 running rough. Against orders, Skipper decided to make emergency landing on Iwo. Could not raise field by radio, night fighter looked us over. Landed 03:50, mortared field as we landed. Stayed on Iwo until 07:30, March 16, 1945, 3 and ½ days. Experience none will forget. I looked for Harold (Cpl. Harold P. Frackelton, Jr., a boyhood chum). He was killed two days before. His buddies, great guys, as were all marines. Flew in engine which we had to change. Larson did a great job. Landed 12:20. CT 11:10. TCT 193:05.
22	March 22, 1945	Chi Chi Jima	Day mission. Target open, first time we had seen it. Nine flack bursts, four right in center of flight, first in a long time. We flew B-3. Take off 11:07. Bombs away 17:03. Landed 20:07. CT 11 hrs. TCT 204:05.
23	March 24, 1945	Marcus	First mission against this rock. No, thank you! It's rough. Gunners just fire for elevation. Island is so small only three planes can go in at a time. U.S. sub on surface about 20 miles off rock to pick up crews of damaged planes. We were C-3. Got over 25 bursts, 5 holes, one about 2 inches from my head, went right on out the top. Babykin really laid them in there, two 1000 lbs. in area 20X60. Take off 07:23. Bombs away 12:20. Landed 18:33. CT 11:10. TCT 215:15. Aircraft: *Sweet Routine*
			Note: After debriefing of mission #23 we grabbed our clothes and took off in transport for Hickham Field, Oahu, Hawaii. We were supposed to have 10 days leave, because of shortage of napalm bombs we were kicked off priority. Stayed on rest 3/26/45 to 4/29/45, best time ever spent in Army. On 5/1/45 we arrived back on Guam.

24	May 9, 1945	Truk	Moen Island. First mission since rest. The kind we like, no flack. All kinds of planes over target, P-51, P-47, B-29, B-17, and B-24s. Good bombing. Babykin laid them in again. Take off 08:00. Bombs away 12:37. Landed 15:35. CT 7:45. TCT 223:00.
*	May 13, 1945	Truk	Fully loaded, 3200 gals of gas, four 1000 lb bombs. Lost #3 on take off just as wheels left ground. Real sweat job, almost mushed in, we all hugged ground when we landed. No credit.
*	May 16, 1945	Marcus	Group navigator got us lost. Weller knew where we were. We should have been in the lead. No credit. CT 11:05. TCT 234:05.
25	May 26, 1945	Marcus	Acted as snooper. Did not carry bombs. Got a good look at island from 4,000 ft. Saw where they hid trucks. CT 10:50. TCT 244:55.
26	June 21, 1945	Truk	Hit Eten Island. #3 in B flight. Flack not bad, saw 5 bursts. Low D flight caught it. Bad weather on return to Guam. First to land, just as field closed in. Planes landed all over island, three crashed, no one hurt. Take off 11:47. Bombs away 16:08. Landed 19:17. CT 7:30. TCT 252:25.
27	June 24, 1945	Marcus	Went after guns. Good bombing, good evasive action. Only heard one burst, flack off and below. Take off 08:05. Bombs away 14:08. Landing 18:45. CT 10:45. TCT 263:10.
			Note: Bombing operations suspended as Group moved from Guam to Okinawa. Ground personnel went by boat, flying crews flew ferrying missions. We flew one and then flew in to stay.

28	July 15, 1945	Usa	First mission out of Okinawa, first against mainland of Japan. Target in northeastern Kyushu. Airfield and dispersal area. 7/10 over target, only saw a few hits. Took 32 P-47s with us, boy did they look good tucked in! They strafed four boats and rail junction. Lost one 150 miles from base on return. I sent in clear for rescue, don't think pilot made it. Nine bursts of flack over target. Take off 07:17. Bombs away 11:20. Landed 15:10. CT 8:10. TCT 271:20.
29	July 17, 1945	Shanghai	First mission to China. Hit airfield northeast of city. Max. strength raid 11th and 494 groups. B-24s, B-25s, A-26s, P-47s, P-51s. 10/10 undercast over target, bombed by radar, no flack. Two planes of 494 went down. One over target, bomb exploded right under plane. Other ditched, crew rescued. Take off 09:15. Bombs away 13:11. Landed 16:04. CT 6:55. TCT 278:15.
30	July 22, 1945	Shanghai	Hit same airfield as on #29, largest in China. Really gave it a plastering. Saw China, very green and very low. Saw muddy waters of the Yangtse. 494th and B-25s went in first. Watched gunfire, fighters strafed, knocked out some. Bombs started large fires. Mac hit but not seriously. Heard 4 bursts all high. Take off 07:40. Bombs away 11:18. Landed 14:12. CT 6:25. TCT 284:40.
31	July 26, 1945	Kikai Shima	Easy one. Island 15 miles east of Amami-0-Shima. Target was Kyushu but fighters not off because of weather. I was only operator to receive orders to abort. Group turned back, 494th did not. Got jumped, lost one. Anderson on 39th. Target between Okie and Kyushu. Take off 08:00. Bombs away 11:35. Landing 13:10. CT 6:35. TCT 291:15.

32	July 29, 1945	Kure	Large naval base on southeastern Honshu, 10 miles south of Hiroshima. Most of Japan's surviving fleet was in harbor. Flew up strait between Kyushu and Shikoku. Max. effort by 7th, 14th and Navy, must have been 1,000 planes in the air. Heavy flack, not accurate, much of it colored (red, green, orange, etc.,) from different ships so gunners could gauge accuracy. Battleship Haruna sunk, all participants claimed a hit. So much action, impossible to give credit to any one plane. Navy probably will get the credit. A big show, clear day. On return flew through flight of Corsairs on strafing dive on crippled cruiser. (Day after mission I was injured and my radio logs were not available to get accurate times for mission.) CT 8:30. TCT 299:45.
			Note: The data for the following five missions are from the memories and records of John Weller and Doyle Ebel.
33	July 31, 1945	Sasebo	On island of Kyushu. A naval port NW of Nagasaki. Weather closed in, fighters had to leave, clouds caused planes to scatter. Elements of 494 joined us. Bombs 3 2000 lbs. Train started on dock area on to carriers. Accurate heavy flack. CT 8:00. TCT 307:45.
34	Aug. 5, 1945	Tarumizi	On island of Kyushu. Large agricultural area. Bomb load twelve 500 lb. fire clusters. Also dropped leaflets telling Japanese people that Russia had joined the Allies; that there was no hope and it was time to surrender. This was one day before first atom bomb was dropped 8/6/45. Plane above dropped full bundle shattered our top turret, knocking out Dick but no serious injury. Fighter escort, accurate flack. Night Mission on right wing took direct hit on bomb run, three chutes. CT 6:20. TCT 314:05.
35	Aug. 7, 1945	Omuto	Kyushu, 38 miles NE of Nagasaki. Industrial center, chemical plants, coke plants, etc. Bomb load eight 1000 lbs. Heavy flack, no enemy fighters. CT 7:00. TCT 321:05.

201

36	Aug. 8, 1945	Iwakuni	Port city on Honshu, rail center and large manufacturing city, 22 miles SW of Hiroshima. Air still dirty and smoky from first atomic bomb three days earlier. Ordered to stay 50 miles from Nagasaki. Return route put us on eastern side of Kyushu. About 11:00 cloud of white smoke rose from Nagasaki area. We reported large fire and major target had been hit. Mushrooming cloud reached high altitude, knew damage was extensive. Our bomb load twelve 500 lb. Fighter cover, accurate flack. CT 8:00. TCT 329:05.
37	Aug. 11, 1945	Kurume	Target 50 miles NE of Nagasaki. Rail center and manufacturing center. Fighter cover, accurate flack. Bombs, twelve 500 lb fire clusters. CT 7:10. TCT 336:15.
	Aug. 12, 1945		Loaded with frag bombs taxied out for take off, jeep from headquarters came out said war over. Taxied back, and CELEBRATED!
			Note: After 8/12/45 flew mission over Japan to see if they were following Armistice. Did not encounter anti-aircraft or resistance. Instructed not to take offensive. Carried ammo, but no bombs. Flying time 6:00.

ACKNOWLEDGEMENTS

I want to recognize and thank the many people who helped me bring this book to reality. John Weller spent many, many hours with me uncovering facts and recounting the many episodes and details of the Jeter Crew's experiences in the Pacific War. Jo Weller was also there providing valuable feedback and making sure we had a nice lunch of soup and sandwiches and a cookie or two.

Doyle Ebel did quite a bit of running around to verify information and to dig up photos for the book. His wife, Pattye, also gave support and helped to pin down facts and contact information. Doyle's daughter, Judy Booth, provided technical assistance and support.

I also want to thank my friend Laura Thomas for her willingness to listen to me when I needed a little push to go forward with the book project. My sisters Ann and Pat also offered encouragement and support. Ann generously absorbed the cost of a long cab ride to visit Dick David in Hoffman Estates, a suburb of Chicago, so I could meet him in person. Pat gave me feedback and enthusiasm for the project that she partly instigated by questions she posed to our dad before he passed away. Cathy listened to me and offered interest and encouragement.

My brother Steve loved to talk to me about the subject of the book because he has a deep curiosity about my dad's war experience. He has shown enthusiasm for the research that fed the book's content and enhanced our understanding of what Army Air Corps pilots had to do and how they lived in the Pacific late in the war. My youngest brother Tim has a strong sense of history and also gave strong moral support. Mike remembered a pertinent story about how my dad, ever the navigator, got out of a truck and consulted the stars when he was lost on a night trip to Oroville from the Bay Area.

I want to thank Grace Provenzano for working so hard to bring the "Jeeter Bug" PBS documentary to fruition. Without the commitment and great work of Grace and her collaborators I would never have learned about and met the men who could paint the picture of what my dad's war experience was like and how it shaped him as a man.

My kids, Joe Paolazzi, Caterina Whiteley and her husband, Justin Whitely, listened to me and said "ooh" and "aah" at all the right intervals, and I thank them for that.

My grandson, Giovanni, wondered throughout the process why it was taking Grammy so long to finish her book. After saying many times: "I need to finish my book," I realized he thought I was *reading* a book, not writing one!

Lastly, I want to acknowledge the help I've received from my work colleagues at Kaiser Permanente Heritage Resources. Lincoln Cushing, who has published five books, kept me on a good path; Bryan Culp was flexible in allowing me vacation time to work on the project.

INDEX

www.ingramcontent.com/pod-product-compliance
Lightning Source LLC
Chambersburg PA
CBHW030529100426

42813CB00001B/196